M2 FD

The
Suffolk
Village Book

The Suffolk Village Book

HAROLD MILLS WEST

With illustrations by Keith Pilling

COUNTRYSIDE BOOKS

NEWBURY BERKSHIRE

First Published 1986
© Harold Mills West 1986
© Illustrations Keith Pilling
All rights reserved. No reproduction
permitted without the prior
permission of the publishers:
Countryside Books
3 Catherine Road, Newbury, Berkshire

ISBN 0 905392 62 0

Cover illustration of Cavendish taken by Mark Mitchels is reproduced by
kind permission of Barbara Hopkinson Books

Produced through MRM (Print Consultants) Ltd., Reading
Typeset by Acorn Bookwork, Salisbury, Wiltshire
Printed in England by J. W. Arrowsmith Ltd., Bristol

Author's note

These are the villages of my native Suffolk. Not every one is listed, since this is no guide or gazetteer but an affectionate summarising of a chosen majority from which, I hope, a sense of the county's spirit and charm can be deduced.

It is a book of peep-holes, looking at people and places past and present and sometimes upon great events that have mingled with humble lives. It is also, I like to think, a wheedling and a cajoling book that will persuade the traveller that there is life beyond the dual-carriage highway and a special charm awaiting any who will turn aside into our quiet by-ways. If anyone can walk more than half a mile along our lanes without coming to a pleasant spot, a clump of trees, a pond or stream or just a gate to lean on, he will be very unlucky indeed. And if he ventures a little further he is bound to come to the church and hall, war memorial and public house of some village, a prospect immediately pleasant while yet being inextricably woven into the past. The threads of a rich tapestry are there for any who care to pick them up. I hope this book may tempt the reader to do so.

I can claim to know the villages of Suffolk very well indeed, for I have spent a vast amount of my more than three score years and ten in the perennial delight of travelling about my own county. I was born in the old town of Woodbridge and before me there were several indigenous generations mostly occupied in some way with the land. Much of my own early life was spent in digging Suffolk soil, an experience which makes me feel slightly proprietorial and indulgent towards those who have never worn dirty boots.

There is no need for me to extol Suffolk. It is being discovered and colonised at a rate that reveals clearly enough the esteem with which it is regarded. Modern-style artists and craftsmen among many others have come to transform and illumine what was in my youth a purely agricultural environment. No doubt the new countrymen could explain their reasons for settling here. Perhaps it is the attraction of fine rivers or the long coastline; perhaps of great churches and village architecture; perhaps of heathland and forest or the sharp, clear winds from the sea. It could be something of all these things. It could also be because an air of innocence still lingers in our villages. After all, that is what most people are searching for.

Harold Mills West
Trimley St. Martin, May 1986

County of SUFFOLK

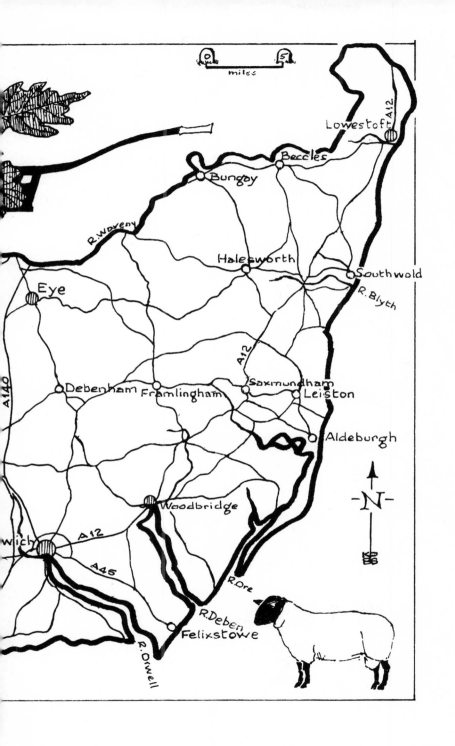

miles

Lowestoft A12

Beccles

Bungay

R.Waveny

Halesworth

Southwold

R.Blyth

Eye

A140

A12

Debenham Framlingham Saxmundham Leiston

Aldeburgh

-N-

Woodbridge

wich A12

A45

R.Ore

R.Deben

R.Orwell Felixstowe

Alderton

Giles Fletcher, the unhappy, uprooted poet and cousin of the famous Elizabethan dramatist braved the cold winds and peasant ignorance of this benighted corner of Suffolk when he was made rector of Alderton by Francis Bacon. Apparently Fletcher found little to his liking either in the place or the people. His scholarship and literary leanings received no encouragement or incentive here and his isolation was believed to be a contributory cause of his early death.

Thomas Fuller remembered Giles Fletcher in a fond obituary: '(Fletcher) at last settled in Suffolk, which hath the best and the worst air in England; best about Bury and worst at the seaside, where Master Fletcher was beneficed. His clownish and low-parted parishioners valued not their pastor according to his worth, which disposed him to melancholy and hastened his dissolution.'

Melancholy this Tudor parson may have been, but others who followed in his footsteps discovered a taste and a fondness for these flat, coastal fields and brisk winds. On the whole, rectors have served their parish with deep and lasting devotion, one surviving in office for 54 years and another for 40 years. With the same dedication, another servant of the church named Cyril George Sherman played the organ here for 58 years without a break except for the bothersome war years. Somewhere hidden in the fallen masonry of the ruined tower is a memorial to another prominent and devoted son of the village, Thurston Whymper, who died at Woodbridge in 1794.

The ancient Suffolk family of Nauntons owned three of the manors here. It was Sir Robert Naunton who became so powerful at the court of Elizabeth that he was widely believed to be the prime mover in the despatch of Sir Walter Raleigh. Adapting quickly to the Stuart regime, he then became Secretary of State under James I and probably amused him greatly with his satirical book: *Fragmenta Regalia or Observations on the late Queen Elizabeth, Her Times and Favourites*.

The light-land fields hereabouts carry potatoes and carrots as well as corn. The area – the triangle between Woodbridge Saxmundham and Orford – was described as the Sandlings by Kirby in his *Suffolk Traveller* of 1829. In his opinion it was the best soil for carrots in the kingdom and had already carried that valuable crop for many centuries.

A well-known local character of the last century, Mrs. Baker, used to be fond of telling yarns in the Swan Inn about her experiences when she was young. One of these was about an unfortunate mix-up when, one dark night and without permission from her mistress, she went out to meet her boy-friend. 'It was as dark as black hogs,' she said. She met her young man and walked with him to Bawdsey. In a shelter there he struck a match and she discovered that she was with the wrong boy. It was something of a calamity, she said, because it had spoiled her chances with the other boy and he earned two shillings more a week!

Aldham

Aldham may not immediately set your blood racing with excitement. The houses, most of them substantial and independent-looking, straggle along the village street and turn to neighbouring Elmsett for the felicity of pub, shop and post office. Yet, if you have an hour to spare on a fine summer's afternoon, take the side road from the village that leads nowhere but to a farm and the church. The church is 'miles away' from the houses but in its vicinity is one of the pleasantest spots you could find in a day's journey. There are low, grazing meadows with a handful of sheep and the hint of a stream and a pond all lying close below the mound on which the round-towered church rests.

Inside the church a wealth of timber stretches almost from floor to roof, so that the occasional visitor, like the regular worshipper, can bask in the warm glow of the polished wood, a welcome contrast to the cold plaster encountered all too often. Outside, footpaths will tempt you into the meadows to savour the balm of this completely tranquil place.

It was not always so. It was near by, on the Common, that the martyr, Dr. Rowland Taylor, was brought to die a terrible death at the stake. He had been dragged from his church in Hadleigh on the orders of Mary Tudor. In the agony of that journey he recovered some momentary curiosity as to his whereabouts and was told he was upon Aldham Common. 'Well, thanks be to God,' he said, 'I am even at home.' A memorial is set there now with the words: 'Anno

Domini 1555. Dr. Taylor, for defending that was good, at this place lost his blood.' On a brass plate in Hadleigh church, the martyr is remembered as: 'An excellent Devyne and Doctor of the Civill Lawe. A preacher rare and fyne.'

Despite the scattered nature of the village, a fine community spirit exists whenever a common interest emerges. A remarkably energetic and concerted effort in 1974, for example, resulted in the surprising achievement of a fourth place in the Britain in Bloom competition. It was close behind the three set-piece villages and ahead of 281 other entrants, a feat almost impossible. Locals who were engaged in the effort still bask, quite properly, in the memory of the most important event since the martyrdom.

Aldringham

This was a smuggler's paradise. It was in the very centre of the trade on this part of the coast, with goods brought in from Thorpeness. The contraband would be carried at night the few miles inland to the village and quickly dispersed from here to the four corners of the county. The base for the illicit trade was the Parrot and Punchbowl Inn but there were cellars and vaults too, dotted about the Common nearby where quantities of rum and gin and brandy could be safely stored. The commerce was extensive and well-organised. One of the smugglers lived in a cottage with an upper window that gave a clear view of the sea and from here signals were sent to the shore to indicate that the way was clear for a run to the Parrot and Punchbowl.

This ancient inn, which flourishes here still, started out long ago as The Case is Altered and over three centuries has absorbed an unmistakable atmosphere from its eventful part in village life. There were occasional sudden raids made upon the inn at the time of the smuggling trade by Excise men assisted by Dragoons and sometimes the law triumphed. The biggest haul ever recorded here was when they swooped on the inn yard at exactly the right moment and found six carts, twelve horses and a total of 300 tubs of gin just being unloaded. The liquor was poured out at once, according to regulations. It flowed across the inn yard and out of the gate and a scene followed like that described by Charles Dickens in *Tale of Two Cities* when a barrel of wine fell from a cart and broke open.

Suddenly the Parrot and Punchbowl became the centre of village activity. Locals arrived as if from nowhere, scooped a hole outside the gate for the gin to flow into and used pails and any containers they could lay their hands on to carry away a mixture of mud and gin. Despite the dilution, it was still so potent that one man died from alcoholic excess that same night.

A famous character of those smuggling days was a Mrs. Gildersleeves, a woman of vast bulk and immense strength, who proved an invaluable aid to the fraternity. It was said that there was many a time when a keg of spirits or a roll of silk or lace would be hidden under her voluminous skirts when the Excise men made a search.

Aspall

Lord Kitchener was proud to add the name of this tiny village to his august titles – 'Viscount Kitchener of Khartoum in the Soudan, of the Vaal in South Africa and of Aspall in the county of Suffolk'. There was a memorable visit from the great man in 1902 when every cottager within walking distance came to cheer and to stare at the first horseless carriage to be seen in these parts.

It was at Aspall Hall that Kitchener's mother was born, a member of that family so long and so closely a part of local history – the Chevalliers. In 1845 Anne Frances Chevallier married Henry Kitchener, left the beautiful moated family house and in Ireland gave birth to the future military hero.

In Aspall, the Chevalliers conceived the extraordinary idea of setting up a cider press in the heart of Suffolk's most conservative agricultural area where there was scarcely an apple tree to be seen for miles. Even more extraordinary, they obviously hoped that it would be a commercial success though it has been suggested since that the only reason for the venture was the Chevallier's own partiality for cider. Whatever the motive, they could scarcely have foreseen that the concern would still be going strong 250 years later.

Aspall cider – Chevallier barley. The synonyms are as familiar as any household names to local people and not unknown to those in far-flung climes. The story of Chevallier barley is told in the *History of Debenham* of 1845 and shows how a little luck and much patience and application can lead to far-reaching results. About the year 1880, we are told, a farm labourer by the name of John

Andrews had been working all day at the threshing of barley. Walking home in the evening he felt some discomfort through the fact that some barley grains had worked their way into his boots. His first task on reaching home was to take his boots off and shake out the offending material. There was part of an ear of barley and several loose grains, all obviously from the same ear. Idly examining what had caused him so much discomfort, he soon realised that the grains were exceptionally large and well-shaped. John Andrews was a thoughtful and conscientious man to whom all aspects of arable farming were of interest. He kept the grains carefully until the spring and then planted them in his garden. There were only three or four shoots that came to an ear but by a further piece of good fortune they were noticed by John Chevallier when he came to the cottage. An enthusiastic agriculturalist, John Chevallier at once saw the possibilities in the situation and the nurturing of the precious seeds rested thenceforward in his hands. For several years the grain was sown over and over again until there was enough to sow an acre. From then on, it had only to be seen to be believed. Chevallier barley spread over the fields and over the county and out over many a field and county far removed from little Aspall.

Assington 🌿

Brampton Gurdon – which could well do for a place-name – was in fact the name of the most prominent member of that expansive seventeenth century family of Assington Hall, the Gurdons. His domestic achievements can still be seen in the church monument where he proudly poses with a wife on each side of him and beside each wife her considerable offspring, in total ten sons and six daughters.

With many other distinguished East Anglian families, the Gurdons chose to fight for Parliament during the Civil War and earned the personal gratitude of Oliver Cromwell, who came to Assington Hall during the siege of Colchester and made his headquarters there. Despite this association, the Gurdons apparently suffered no slight or retribution from the Royalists after the Restoration. Another domestic record was made by Brampton's eldest son who died in 1679 after 55 years of married bliss.

In August 1957, fire broke out at the Hall. When the brigade arrived the fire was well advanced and an inadequate water supply made the final catastrophe inevitable. The Hall was completely destroyed. A looker-on summed it all up in Suffolk style. 'That was a rare owd blaze' he said.

Barham

William Kirby, the naturalist, was an incumbent here for 68 years. He was born a few miles away at Witnesham Hall and as a young man with Oxford behind him he walked one summer's evening to Barham to view the parish that was to be his. He found it 'a snug place for a young fellow to step into'. Snug indeed he must have concluded it to be since only the grave finally separated him from the village. Perhaps Kirby was the completely happy man — comfortably embowered in the insect-buzzing countryside of the 18th century and with the leisure to follow his abiding interest in observing all that was around him. He would surface from a study of some insect or plant only long enough to write a monograph for the Royal Society and then become absorbed again in the endless mysteries of instincts and behaviour in the creature world. In 1818 he was elected Honorary President of the newly-formed Entomology Society.

BARHAM MANOR

He was not the only one of the Kirby clan to attain distinction. As well known, perhaps, was John Kirby of Halesworth, the writer and topographer. His son John found fame as a painter and as a close friend of Thomas Gainsborough.

Not so fortunate in worldly affairs were the inmates of that Victorian house of gloom, the dark and forbidding-looking Barham work-house. This House of Industry has often been referred to as Oliver Twist's work-house. People have declared — such is the power of fiction — that it was in this very building that Oliver actually asked for more. There is no doubt that Dickens saw this work-house when visiting Suffolk but probably he saw a great many others too as there was no shortage of such places at that time.

Social historians may well wonder at the juxtaposition of Barham work-house with the vast estate and mansion just across the road. This is Shrubland Park whose imposing gatehouses that hide the long drives to the house must be something like a mile apart. In earlier times this Palladian mansion was the home of the powerful Bacon family and then the Middletons. Sir William Middleton was an M.P. and High Sheriff of Suffolk. The Barham church provided for such importance by raising a front pew on four steps and ensuring that it was adequately cushioned and screened from the common gaze.

In the present century Shrubland Park has been occupied by the de Saumerez family and a few years ago the house with necessary additions was transformed by Lord and Lady de Saumerez into a rest place for the world-weary — a sauna and health farm.

The handsome parish church stands upon the side of a hill encompassed with trees. Here the venerable old rector, Kirby, spent his happy years and there was a particular old cedar tree in whose shade he loved to sit and ponder on the wonders of the natural world. Not far beyond the church is Barham Manor, standing a little back from the road and for many years the home of the literary Hadfields. In the years after the war it was a delight to look through the gate and see peacocks strutting on the lawn.

Barningham 🦢

There were three manors here, the most important one Barningham Hall Manor owned by John de Montfort in the 14th century. It then passed to the Barninghams, to the Edens and was then purchased by Maurice Barrow. A flagstone in the church extols the virtues of his wife and tells us that she was the daughter of Sir Richard Smith of Leeds in Kent and was a widow already when she married Barrow.

Both husband and wife died in 1666, a circumstance that asks to be associated with the Plague, though this is not known. Barrow bequeathed Barningham Hall to his cousin Maurice Shelton, first of a succession of Sheltons and most of them called Maurice. The last Maurice was a man of some literary pretensions who brought out an exhausting two-volume work called *Essay on Nobility*. Its success was short-lived.

The 14th century church is of a modest size but offers a rich expanse of warm-looking timber within. It includes panelling along the walls of the nave, and an oak reredos and oak font cover, both cunningly carved. The pulpit has a clerk's desk below on which, during the last century, the pious James Wright sat for 52 years.

Towards the end of the 18th century there was a fire which all but destroyed the village. It started in the kitchen of a baker's shop, soon spread through the house and was carried in a fresh breeze to the cottages nearby. With dry thatch and timber for fuel the flames next engulfed a farmhouse and buildings, then the Parsonage House and seriously threatened the church.

'It catched fire three several times but was providentially saved,' says the account. It was not so providential for the village people for five families lost their homes that day.

Barrow

Barrow, or Barou as it was once called, was originally the property of the Crown. A thousand years ago it belonged to Edward the Confessor and was duly included in the Conqueror's possessions in the Domesday Book. Richard I made a wedding present of all Barrow's land and rights to the Earl of Pembroke on his marriage. Several changes of ownership followed until the 16th century, when the Heigham family took over.

Somehow the Heighams, whose name was taken from the nearby village of Higham, managed to secure respect from both sides during the religious differences of the Tudors. Sir Clement Heigham rallied to the cause of Queen Mary at her accession and was made

Speaker of the House of Commons. In due course his son, Sir John, was just as energetic for Elizabeth when she acceded. When the Armada threatened, he was appointed to command a Suffolk band of infantry and a grateful queen halted a progress through the countryside to visit him at Barrow Hall.

In this century, Barrow has known changes of fortune. Around 1953 a howl of anguish went up when it was realised that the healthy population total of the 1900s had been reduced by a quarter and forecasts suggested that the village would stagnate. In fact, all such pessimism has been completely overturned by events, to such an extent that Barrow has been described in recent years as the liveliest village in Suffolk. It may well be. Its list of activities is impressive, with organisations and societies enough to include every last parishioner and a record of communal achievement that many could learn from. The transformation is due chiefly to the numbers of newcomers who have set up homes here since the war, who have taken the village to their hearts and used their energy and new ideas for the benefit of all.

New houses and old make a good mix and the spacious green is a focal point for many of them. There is one house called the Gables but often referred to as the Doll's House which catches the eye simply because it is a tall, rather odd-shaped building with no known purpose in its design. It is generally accepted as a folly. On the edge of the village is Broom's Barn Farm, a 200-acre research station which has been devoted entirely to the study of sugar-beet, the only such centre in the country.

Barsham

There is a City here — strangely enough, for there is no street, no single pub, not even a post office. There is, however, a row of cottages which earned this title at some point and the name sticks.

Barsham provides me with some of my earliest memories. There were hot, summer days when we would walk down the long, sandy 'loke' to the mill and the river and we would lie on the footbridge to watch the clouds of minnows in the water and listen to the endless sighing of the rushes. The marshes beside the Waveney are never completely silent but are always mysterious and sometimes ghostly. Like all boys at that time I was irresistibly drawn to the clicking sound of a self-binder in the fields at harvest and would follow the machine as it went round and round the standing corn, throwing out the tied sheaves that would have to be stood up in 'shocks'. Boys would stand around with sticks waiting for the rabbits to run from their diminishing hiding-place. On one occasion I killed a rabbit myself with a knobbed stick as it came out of the corn. It was my first and my last.

The Sucklings, to whom there are many references in the village in one form or another, were lords of the manor and also supplied a long succession of incumbents of the parish church. Famous above all of them is the name of Catherine Suckling, who was born at Barsham Rectory in 1725, the daughter of the Rev. Maurice Suckling, for she was the mother of Nelson the hero of Trafalgar.

Her brother, Captain Maurice Suckling, whose naval exploits were inevitably overshadowed by those of his brilliant nephew, nevertheless earns some mention, for it was he who encouraged Nelson in his childhood, taught him seamanship and discipline and set an example as a gallant commander.

Sir John Suckling has a place in the literary annals of the 17th century as the Poet Laureate, though this title gives only a sober picture of a man more distinguished as a warrior and – when there was no fighting to be done – as a gambler and notorious wild man of contemporary society. As often as not, Sir John was in conflict with the authorities over some indiscretion or other. On one occasion, after a particularly dubious series of adventures in Europe, he was hauled before the fearsome Court of the Star Chamber.

Somehow, he charmed himself out of that corner and was allowed to go free, one of the few to survive the experience. Afterwards, he considered it wise to give himself a lower profile, as we say nowadays and retired for a time to settle quietly at Barsham Hall and write poetry. Among the more quotable of his lines are these:

'Out upon it, I have loved Three whole days together,
And am like to love three more, If it prove fair weather.'

It was not long before Sir John's love of dangerous living brought him out of retirement to ally himself to a new cause. This time it was a hare-brained scheme to rescue the impeached Earl of Strafford before he could be executed. Unfortunately, the plot was discovered and he was forced to leave the country hurriedly and live in France, where he spent the rest of his days in unhappy exile.

The Holy Trinity church with its grand porch and Jacobean interior stands in a pleasant setting overlooking park-like fields. Within the church lies that most powerful lord of the manor, Sir Robert Atte Tye the Younger and his mother, Dionysia. His father, Sir Robert Atte Tye the Elder was that most thoughtful man who ordered that four dozen bottles of wine should be provided and consumed at his graveside during the interment.

Barton Mills 🦌

In old writings this is Barton Togryng (Two-grind), referring to the presence of two mills. One of them was a water mill situated on the Lark river and the other a windmill which ultimately retired from profitable use while the water mill was still going strong.

Prominent in the Barton Mills story, past and present, is the Bull Inn. Because of its position on the established coaching routes it was of more than usual importance in the travelling world of the 18th century, particularly for the wealthy patrons of the turf at Newmarket. It was, as the Bull Inn itself proclaimed – 'the annual resort of the Nobility and Gentry in the sporting season.' Among the distinguished guests it made welcome was the young Victoria who travelled that way just before her accession.

Parson Woodforde stayed there on many occasions and in his diary of April 13th 1775 he described the journey he had just taken from London to his home in Norfolk. It is a chastening thought to those of us who grumble at modern travelling conditions to be told of the vicissitudes of his journey and then to be cheerfully informed – 'these are the best roads I ever travelled.'

Setting off from the Turks Head in the Strand in the early morning in a coach and four horses, he reached the Bull-Faced Stagg at Epping Forest in good time. The horses were swiftly changed and the coach rumbled on as far as Harlow. Here he changed to a chaise and a fresh set of horses for the journey to Newmarket, where he dined. The day's travel was far from over, however, for he then took another chaise to the Bull at Barton Mills, another to Thetford and so to Attleborough, where he thanked God to have arrived safely at 11 p.m. Considering the distance, the changes of horses and vehicles, the state of the roads and the many hazards of such a journey, a degree of gratitude for arrival must surely be appropriate.

Battisford ✍

Merchants and bankers may do much to change peoples' lives but they seldom make the history books. That prince of entrepreneurs, Sir Thomas Gresham, performed immense feats in business and finance for three of the Tudor monarchs but would not stand comparison with the adventurers of the period. His name does persist in the form of a famous college which was originally his own London home and in the specialised history of the City of London.

'Gresham? Gresham? Something to do with the Royal Exchange,' said my least favourite nephew, who knows everything. He was right, of course. 'Something to do with the Royal Exchange', sums up the general knowledge of Gresham's work. In fact, of course, he founded and built the original Exchange but this was probably of less importance at the time than his financial activities on behalf of the crown.

To be sure, Sir Thomas was born with a silver spoon in his mouth and an instinct for business. He was the son of a lord mayor, descendant of a wealthy dynasty and owner of vast estates. One of them, his favourite retreat from the affairs of the royal and national purse, was at Battisford. Short and sweet were his visits to the estate for his shrewd knowledge of merchant banking had brought him to the notice of the king and he had been appointed to the exacting post of agent to his majesty. The king was Henry VIII, a monarch notoriously prodigal with wealth and many and devious were the ways in which Gresham sought to fill that ever clutching hand. As a giant among entrepreneurs, he travelled constantly in Europe, raising loans and delaying their repayment, buying and selling merchandise at great profit, taking part in the lucrative arms smuggling trade, engaging in all kinds of trickery and bribery if that were necessary to secure funds for his royal master. Since he was so completely involved in these lawful and unlawful manipulations of vast sums of money, his own affairs benefited and his fortune grew even larger. He owned a palace in Antwerp, his country estate at Battisford and houses in Sussex, Middlesex, Norfolk and London.

Gresham's outstanding association with Battisford lay in the building of the Royal Exchange. The timber came from his own woods here and the frame of the building was partly assembled on the village common before being carried on his farm waggons on the long journey to London. That the Exchange was lost in the Fire of London does not diminish Gresham's enterprise in initiating this gathering of merchants under one roof.

Clever and diplomatic as he undoubtedly was, he kept the Tudor monarchs happy and his popularity high all through the reigns of Henry VIII, Edward VI, Mary and well into the sovereignty of Elizabeth. It was his great pride that he was able to entertain the Queen as lavishly as any eastern potentate and perhaps the greatest moment of his life was when she performed the opening ceremony at the completion of his Royal Exchange.

Bedingfield

Somehow, there still seems to linger a faint odour of feudalism in some villages where the manor was held by one family for a long period of time. The seigneur may have been completely benevolent and not oppressive but there was always the requirement of allegiance and respect from village folk. In such places as Helmingham, Wingfield and Bedingfield, for example, that certain atmosphere remains and in my fancy there are scattered houses that look all ready to touch their hats to a passing lord and master.

Bedingfield lies a little to the north of Debenham in good agricultural land and no doubt more interested in modern farming matters than in village history but it would be impossible to avoid completely the family name of Bedingfield. After all, on one brass alone in the church are the names of 15 Bedingfields, most of them distinguished in one way or another. This extensive family once formed so close a kinship with the village that the names are almost synonymous and whether the Bedingfields gave their name to the village or the other way round is of no importance.

Originally from Norfolk, the Bedingfields had their seat here for something like 500 years altogether, living for much of the time at moated Flemings Hall. The manor was first held by Snape Priory and was granted to Cardinal Wolsey as a gift towards the endowment of his proposed college in Ipswich. Wolsey seems to have done well out of such donations at the time of the Dissolution. Unfortunately the college idea foundered when the Cardinal was deposed and the manor was then given to the Duke of Norfolk, soon after coming into the possession of the Bedingfields.

Benacre

It is a place to hear about, to pay one's respects to, but hardly ever to visit. In a way it deserves to be known much better for this must surely be the nursery of Suffolk agriculture in the present century. It would not be too extravagant to compare the dedicated work at Benacre Hall with that done by Coke of Holkham in Norfolk in the eighteenth century. That the results at Holkham were more spectacular was simply because there was then so much more scope for improvements. In the present century, less so, but there has been the same enthusiasm for the cause and the furtherance of agricultural science and good husbandry particularly within the home county.

Sir Robert Gooch was perhaps the best known and most tireless farmer in the long line of Gooch's at Benacre Hall. The estate was purchased for the family by Bishop Gooch in 1745 and it covers a huge expanse of land between the A12 and the sea, where constant erosion has taken place. Sir Robert's main concern was to foster the cause of the three indigenous breeds of Suffolk farm animals. In the case of the black-faced Suffolk sheep there is no doubt of their success, while the handsome Punch heavy horse is still loved and thriving so far as mechanisation allows. But, from observation alone, I would say that few farmers nowadays favour the Red Poll, though it was once given much prominence because of its dual purpose in providing both milk and beef.

Long before Benacre Hall was built, the manor here was owned and occupied by the immensely powerful line of the Dacres, peers of the realm and friends of kings. It was the ninth Lord Dacre who was entrusted with the delicate task of welcoming the German bride of Henry VIII, Ann of Cleves. Since the king had not seen her, it must have been a disconcerting discovery to Dacres that the lady was plain and unbecoming. Dacres escorted her to London in some trepidation that he might excite the wrath of the king for not bringing the beautiful bride he expected. It was, no doubt, an occasion for leaving the royal presence as hurriedly as possible, once the two had met.

Unfortunately, Lord Dacres was to meet a worse fate than kingly disapproval, as it turned out. Young and adventurous, a hot-headed gallant among similar contemporaries, he sometimes engaged in dangerous escapades. There was one night when he joined with other young scions of noble families to go on a chase about the grounds of a great house in Sussex, where he was a guest. The chase extended into the park and woodland with a good deal of noise but probably held nothing more sinister than the excitement of a wild ride in the dark. Gamekeepers heard the noise and suspected poachers, made a sudden attack on the young men and a great battle ensued. At the end, one of the gamekeepers was found to be dead, Dacre was tried for murder, received no help from the king and was found guilty. His estates were forfeited but were later returned to his successor, the tenth Lord Dacres. He himself was hanged at the Tyburn Tree.

Benhall

One of the surprises in the study of village life is the extent to which the gentry and lords of the manor looked after their own parishes, not only in bequeathing funds for the aged and the poor but also in providing for the schooling of the young. Compulsory state education did not arrive until 1870 but there were few villages without some form of voluntary schooling long before that.

As far back as 1731, Sir Edward Duke left £1000 for the education of the children of Benhall. Apparently a quarter of this sum was sufficient to build a school with a master's house alongside and to provide a playground and garden. The £750 remaining was invested and the income used to pay the schoolmaster to teach reading, writing and arithmetic to all the poor children of the parish. A hundred years later another benefactor, Edward Hollond of Benhall Lodge, updated the facility by leaving money to repair the school and raise the teacher's salary. Soon after, another member of this family, the Rev. E. Hollond, erected a National School on Benhall Green which was immediately attended by 60 boys and 55 girls — a very healthy number of voluntary pupils anxious to read and write.

This homely village spreads itself in good farming country just short of Saxmundham. Like a naughty child its offshoot of Benhall

Green lies a mile or so away, also split from the parent by reason of the busy main road. To take a short trip along the narrow lane to the Green is to sense a little of the old-style village life and this is repeated further on in the Sandy Lane of neighbouring Sternfield. Returning to Biggs Corner by the Sternfield road gives an excuse for another look at the church and its approach. This short, leafy avenue of oaks and beeches on one side and firs on the other makes a suitable introduction to the beautiful church mantled in trees and, in summer, with roses about the door. Beside the churchyard a plantation of poplars whisper above the peaceful graves.

Bentley ✍

This was the original home of the ancient family of Tollemaches, said to have arrived in this country even before the Norman Conquest. Tollemaches were lords of the manor and received the advowson of the church and two large woods called Portland Grove and New Grove at the time of the Dissolution. When the family moved to Helmingham their seat here and all their properties were retained so that Bentley and Helmingham became twin bases for the Tollemache dynasty.

Before the suppression of religious houses, there was a small community of Black Canons at Dodnash Priory, about two miles south west of the village. When dispersed, the Priory was given to Cardinal Wolsey (who seems to have been a most proficient receiver of presents from all quarters). The gift was intended to assist with the cost of Wolsey's abortive project to found a college in Ipswich. There is still a Dodnash Priory Farm on the original site.

Not far from the edge of this quiet village lies the large and wandering expanse of the Alton Reservoir, some three miles long and reaching almost to the river Stour.

Blundeston ✍

This village belongs to Suffolk and not Norfolk by the skin of its teeth and we duly add the name to our many villages with literary associations. Modern pilgrims inspired by the printed word turn up at Blundeston from time to time, trying to identify some of the features described so memorably in David Copperfield. The round-towered church particularly earns attention as well as the house known in the book as the Rectory but nowadays called the Rookery.

'I was born at Blunderstone, in Suffolk,' David is made to say and later he speaks of the church with its high-backed pews where Peggotty tried to keep his attention from wandering during the sermon.

Happily, it is the sort of village which one can easily imagine could have seen the young David playing in the churchyard – 'there is nothing half so green as I know anywhere,' he declares later, 'as the grass of that churchyard; nothing so shady as its trees; nothing half so quiet as its tombstones.' It is the sort of place where Barkis becomes immediately credible and could be just around the corner urging 'the laziest horse in the world' to pull the carrier's cart. Miss Betsy Trotwood could come flurrying down the road at any time and present herself autocratically at the door of the old Rectory. Blundeston is content not to outgrow Dickens.

It is said that the writer saw the name Blundeston on a signpost as he was walking from Yarmouth to Lowestoft and later misspelled the name. More likely the change to Blunderstone was a deliberate elaboration since it is completely in tune with Dickens' obvious delight in odd-sounding names, a delight that readers share.

The village carries another rather tenuous literary thread, for the poet Gray used often to come to the Lodge here to visit his friend Norton Nicholls. Modern travellers are lodged well at The Plough Inn and can be forgiven if they avoid that large factory-like building not far away that is distinctly un-Dickensian and is in fact one of Britain's most up-to-date 'nicks'.

Blythburgh

This is one of the great churches of the county, with an added power and beauty from its position overlooking the low-lying coastal flats – 'the cathedral of the marshes' it has been called. Rich merchants subscribed to the building of it and it forms an impressive monument to those who lived and traded here when Blythburgh flourished. Though it is tempting to compare it with the great churches of Suffolk wool towns, this comparison is only valid as to

BLYTHBURGH CHURCH

26

size. Wool had no part in the wealth here, and the town's importance came by way of the river Blyth. Shipbuilding went on here and a great deal of fishing. For a long time Blythburgh was undoubtedly a most prosperous town. It was, as Thomas Gardner tells us – 'the residence of merchants and reputable people'.

Now only the church remains to hint at the glory of long ago. Like nearby Dunwich, the town completely disappeared, not into the sea in this case but into decay and disuse. The life-blood of commerce that came by the river was halted when the river Blyth became choked and unnavigable. The town lived on for a time as a ghostly shadow of its former self, then a succession of destructive fires assured its end.

Those merchants who knew Blythburgh well at its greatest and most prominent time must have turned in their graves when, early in the 19th century it was decided to build a workhouse here. Perhaps there was some of that pioneering spirit left in the area for this particular House of Industry inspired hate and resentment from the start. There was talk of prison-like conditions and harsh treatment of honest folk whose only crime was to be poor.

On August 5th 1765, a gathering of several hundred men marched to the new workhouse intent on destroying it. Their plea was that they should be allowed to work in the fields and share the harvest payment as true countrymen rather than be taken over, body and soul, by the Union. Soldiers were sent for to disperse the rioters and in a fierce battle one man was killed and six taken away to Ipswich gaol.

The incident had some effect on the authorities, for soon after, public assurances were given as to conditions in the workhouse. 'Good new Feather Beds will be provided,' it was promised. 'Beds may be brought in by inmates provided they are Clean'. Also, married couples would have their own separate bedrooms but 'disorderly or Lewd persons will be punished by an Abatement of Diet'. The Victorians were ever masters of euphemism.

A mile or so away from the village, where bracken and furze inhabit the soil, stands Blythburgh Lodge, or Westwood Lodge as it was once called, built long ago by a despotic landowner whose ghost is supposed to haunt the corridors still. Certainly in that lonely situation the house looks a likely sort of place for a ghost. Apparently the old squire had been a great horseman and a hunting man and after his untimely death continued to ride an invisible horse in the corridors at night. A more appealing ghost reputedly seen on many occasions was a young damsel in a long dress. Vigils have been organised on many occasions to catch a sight of her but ghosts seldom appear when required.

A more credible story, perhaps, is that of a lorry driver who careered off the road not far from the Lodge, having been confronted, he said, by two figures in the road. A man in cloak and knee breeches was holding the reins of a black horse while a little girl in a poke bonnet was holding on to the man's arm. When the driver jumped out of his cab there was no one to be seen.

Botesdale 🍂

Botesdale – the dale of St. Botolph – lies each side of the road about two thirds of the way from Bury St. Edmunds to Diss. Houses and shops huddle close beside the long street which extends so far that at certain points not immediately obvious it runs into the territory or the neighbouring villages of Rickinghall Superior and Rickinghall Inferior.

A weekly market was allowed here during the Middle Ages and a fair to celebrate St. Botolph's Day on the 18th May. Such excitements as this may have contributed to the profligate conduct of a young gentleman named Robert Bacon, of the wealthy and ubiquitous Bacon family, who became the classic bad-egg, the bounder and cynic who boasted that he could scarcely wait to squander his promised inheritance. Some may have seen it as a well-deserved fate that he did not inherit at all, since he died before his father, perhaps of sheer ennui.

An earlier Bacon, Sir Nicholas, an undoubted goody of the family, obtained permission from Queen Elizabeth to build and maintain a Grammar School here, an innovation well ahead of the times. The school flourished for over two centuries, providing suitable education for the sons of local gentry and farmers and turning out some distinguished characters including Hablet Browne (Phiz) the illustrator and John Fenn, the publisher of the Paston Letters. When the school came to an end, having apparently outlived its usefulness, the income was used to provide local boys with Bacon scholarships to other schools. The building changed its role and became a 'Chapel of Ease'.

Three hundred and fifty years ago, mischievous young boys of the early school occupied odd moments in carving their names or initials on the beams. Some can be seen still. The oldest is that of William Swyer, aged eleven, who in 1609 gouged out for himself a name that he could never have imagined would still be read in the twentieth century.

Boulge

The best thing – in fact, the only thing – to do at Boulge is to visit the church. The village itself is almost non-existent. The church, however, shelters the grave of Edward Fitzgerald, the poet and translator of Omar Khayyam, who lived here in the village for an important sixteen years of his life and nearby for almost the whole of it. When his family moved from Bredfield to Boulge Hall, he set up his own home in the Lodge which stood in the Hall grounds. Here, comfortably ensconced with his books, a housekeeper to look after him, he alternately grumbled and enthused about the rustic life he was leading. 'One of the dullest places in England' he decided on one occasion but on another – 'there is not nor ever was such a country as old England.'

Fitzgerald was a familiar figure for miles around for even when he moved from Boulge (we locals usually pronounce it Bowage) to Woodbridge about three miles away, he tramped the same familiar roads. At Woodbridge he took lodgings on the Market Hill for about thirteen years, not far from the beloved river and his yacht, the Scandal. Here he could meet more frequently his cronies and literary friends for discussions and carousels. The house where he lived can be identified now by his initials high up on the wall. The only cloud in his life here was his unfortunate marriage but this interrupted his freedom-loving days for only a short period before they separated. His delight was to travel – not far, by modern measures, but frequently – to his favourite places in Suffolk, particularly Lowestoft. When distinguished friends like Thomas Carlyle came to see him, he would whisk them off to such places so that they could share his enjoyment. His wanderings were constant and meditative to the extent that he often forgot the reason for going.

'How did I get here?' he wrote from Lowestoft in 1841. 'Why, I left Geldeston yesterday to go to Norwich. Now the coach has stopped here by the sea. I am quite satisfied. I feel that I cannot reasonably expect it to go any further – so here I have spent the day. Like a naughty schoolboy, I won't go home to Geldeston just yet.'

Geldeston, on the Waveney, was another of Fitzgerald's favourite visiting places. His sister lived there and fussed over him, knowing that on his own he had little thought for his own comfort. On one occasion when he arrived at Geldeston he admitted to feeling a trifle queer. He had been walking too long in the sun, he said, then eaten too many unripe peaches and had gone to sleep lying in long wet grass.

A contemporary description of the wandering poet and translator says: 'I often saw this old gentleman wandering or rather drifting abstractedly about the country lanes in an ill-fitting suit with a cap on the back of his head, blue spectacles on nose and an old cape cast anyhow about his shoulders. Few figures were more familiar to me by sight, few less regarded; and many a time must my pony's hoofs have spattered this forlorn-looking figure as we cantered past him in the neighbouring lanes.'

Bradfield Combust

It was just Bradfield before the Combust took place in 1327, when it suffered in the attacks made upon various religious houses belonging to the abbey of Bury. Frustration and anger at the growing wealth of the abbey at the expense of poor people aroused a considerable rebellion in that year against the power of the Abbot. He was not only a spiritual lord but in effect a baron over temporal affairs. He could appoint the town aldermen as well as clergy and anywhere within a mile of the town he had the authority of a supreme magistrate with power to inflict the death sentence. Moreover, no official of the king could operate in this area without his permission.

Little wonder, perhaps, that 20,000 aggrieved local people followed aldermen and burgesses of the town to set fire to the monastery, having recovered masses of valuables secured there. The same treatment was accorded to the Hall at Bradfield, which, together with the lordship, belonged to the abbey. The rebels were

30

BRADFIELD COMBUST
OLD FORGE & ANTIQUES.

later punished by the king, with about 30 cart-loads of prisoners being carried off to Norwich gaol and another 200 outlawed.

When the Hall was rebuilt it became in due course the home of Bradfield's most notable resident, Arthur Young. When his father died he took over the farm here, added 40,000 larches and oaks to the fine avenue of limes his father had planted and then engaged himself energetically in the particular role he set himself in agriculture. It was a time of great change in farming methods, with people like Tull, Bakewell and 'Turnip' Townshend making obsolete many of the ways of old. It was Arthur Young who led and brought together all the experiments and achievements in records and information that ultimately made the basis of his great and lasting work, *The Annals of Agriculture*.

Bramfield

Nowadays the busy A144 carries the majority of travellers summarily through Bramfield and onward the 3 miles or so to Halesworth but for those who pause here there is reward enough. Once there were two wonders to gaze at, but time has finally defeated the famous Bramfield Oak, believed to have been a thousand years old and a fair stripling when Alfred was king. It is spoken of in ancient rhymes; that ubiquitous queen, Elizabeth, sheltered under its branches and many a Suffolk cottager walked a few miles just to stare and wonder at the magnificent old tree. It held on to life with the grace and tenacity of an aged monarch and died with dignity, dropping its last three branches on a completely calm day in 1843.

The other phenomenon is still very visible — the round tower apparently belonging to the church of St. Andrew but standing aloof some 20 feet away from the main building. The first impression that there might have been some aberration or mistake in the building of the church is soon dispelled. The tower was erected a century before the church at a time when powerful barons were at each other's throats and it was intended for defence, a modest fortress against possible attack. The only other disassociated church tower is at Beccles.

The village has been more than usually well endowed with grants and charities by local gentry. An almshouse for the poor was provided for in the will of Thomas Neale in 1701, money was given by others for the teaching of children to read, for free bibles, for the erection of an Independent Chapel costing £250. Other bequests cared for repairs to the almshouses, for school books and teaching fees. The £80 left by Elizabeth Archer was invested in a house and 10 acres of land whose rent was for the relief of the poor. The first school was built and maintained by local people. It makes an impressive catalogue of self-help and generosity in the 18th and 19th centuries.

There seems to have been nothing sweet, however, about the originator of the remarkable epitaph on a gravestone here on Bridget Applethwaite, who died in 1737. It was someone undoubtedly of advanced feministic views who saw Bridget as something of a martyr who, 'after the fatigue of a married life, borne by her with incredible patience, and after the enjoyment of the glorious freedom of an early and unblemished widowhood, resolved to run the risk of a second marriage, but death forbade the banns.'

Bramford 🦢

The spreading tentacles of Ipswich have almost dragged this growing community into the borough but the village stubbornly holds on to its separate identity. It is certainly worth-while to do so for it is a very attractive spot which retains an aura of old-style self-dependence.

The church spire catches the eye from far off. It is a leaded spire added in the 18th century to the square tower built 400 years earlier. Perhaps there was a good array of craftsmen here at that time or the church was exceptionally well-loved, for there is a wealth of carving in stone and wood both inside and out. The appointments of the interior are rare. A 14th century chancel screen of stone still shows the masons marks, a tiny thread that seems to link the past more closely to the present. There is a more modern reredos screen, beautifully carved and an alms pillar which, with the elaborate font cover, seems to date from the Tudor period.

Close by the church runs the sluggish river Gipping, still the focal point of the village and a rendezvous for young and old on summer days but no longer the useful waterway that it was. Once barges regularly came up here from Ipswich and even continued beyond to

Stowmarket. Now the mill and the large fertiliser plant beside the river are served by other means of transport.

Edward Byles Cowell was a Bramford man who followed a distinguished career as an oriental scholar. His claim to fame, however rests solely on the fortuitous discovery in the Bodleian Museum at Oxford of the manuscripts of Omar Khayyam. A happy decision made him send a copy to his friend Edward Fitzgerald, who set to work at once on the memorable translation.

Brandeston 🌿

There was witchcraft at Brandeston, so it was said, in the 17th century. Matthew Hopkins, the witch-hunter smelled it out immediately with his long nose. His accusing hand pointed to the frail old clergyman, a victim easy to subdue. The Rev. John Lowes had officiated here in the 14th century church for fifty long years and but for the hysteria about witches and the black arts, might have lived out his last few years in contentment. As it was, he became yet another sacrifice to ignorance and superstition. When he was accused of sending imps to do evil deeds he agreed that he had done so. At his trial at Bury St. Edmunds he was found guilty and made to perform his own burial service. He was hanged there, with no one having the wit or the courage to protest, in 1646.

In contrast to this tale of misfortune is the story of the remarkable career of another son of Brandeston. This was the famous lawyer, Charles Austin, the subject of open admiration by such distinguished figures as Macaulay and John Stuart Mill. He was born in 1799 at Creeting Mill. When his family moved to Brandeston, the boy's intellectual qualities were noted and he was sent to Norwich to learn to become a surgeon but his own inclination was more and more towards the study of law. In due course Austin became 'the first lawyer in England' and renowned for his oratory and conversational powers. For all that, having made a fortune and after refusing the post of Solicitor-General, he came back to Brandeston Hall to live quietly for the rest of his life.

Brandeston Hall was built in the reign of Edward VI by Andrew Revett who had purchased the manorial rights. His descendants were to live there for 300 years. It was soon after their departure that the Hall was almost destroyed by fire but was eventually restored in keeping with the original. At the end of the Second World War the Hall was bought by Framlingham College for use as a junior school.

Brightwell

There was a time when the little tributary flowed right across the road in this beautiful valley below the church. Coming down the hill from Martlesham with the church high in the trees on the left and the woods – full of bluebells in the spring – on the right, it is only the insistence of traffic that prevents one from pausing here. When I was young there was no such compulsion. On the earliest journey that I can remember, by horse and trap from Woodbridge to Felixstowe with Brightwell at the half-way point, it was a place to pause and let the pony stand in the water to drink.

Sir Thomas Essington saw the beauty of the little valley and built his mansion here in the 17th century. It was considered 'a very faire house built of brick', which scarcely does justice to the palatial scale of that edifice with its noble proportions surrounded by beautiful gardens, secluded walks and arbours. Sir Thomas was lord of the manor and generous to the parish and those about him but was ill-rewarded by fate. In the church are two sad inscriptions, one to Anne, his daughter, 'whom God tooke out of this life'. Her age is spelled out with painful exactitude. 'But seventeen years, five moneths and seventeen dayes'. The other monument is to his son aged five.

Another son inherited the estate and soon sold it to Sir Samuel Barnadiston, a Sheriff of Suffolk who had managed to keep both sides happy during the Civil War. The place changed hands again quite quickly and within a hundred years of its erection, this huge estate and imposing mansion was demolished. Nothing remains. Afterwards, a farmhouse was built on the site. It was an unhappy place for everyone connected with it and makes one wonder if it was a good idea to build on the marshy lands there, attractive though they are.

It was Sir Thomas Essington who rescued the church from advanced decay and neglect, who rebuilt the tower and restored the nave. The square tower looks slightly odd because instead of being a separate vertical structure in its own right, it appears to sprout from the roof.

Bromeswell

For most people who pass this way, which must include a good proportion of U.S. servicemen going to and from the nearby base, the name Bromeswell means the Cherry Tree Inn. The village itself manages to remain completely camouflaged and hidden from the main road and the rare visitor will find that it has another defence against strangers. The narrow roads that lead you through this charming little settlement of houses form a kind of horse-shoe shape so that you are soon tipped out again into the busy road about half a mile from where you entered. The 'front' that the Cherry Tree offers to the passer-by represents more strategy. It provides for the hungry and thirsty and sends them onward so contented that they seldom want to trespass on to the quiet roads of the village.

I do not blame Bromeswell at all. It likes to keep itself to itself. It also takes a proprietorial interest in the stretch of the river Deben that wanders this way from Wilford Bridge. The river here is only a few yards wide and much of that clogged up with reeds and rushes but it is possible to walk for some distance along the banks.

It may well be the sort of place where romance flourishes. A stone in the churchyard points out a sad love story that once unfolded here. The couple were Robert Manly and Mary King and the year 1822 when they were joined in their final union. Mary was not strong and her health declined as the young lovers prepared for their wedding. When it became inevitable that she would die, Mary revealed her dread of grave-robbers who at that time earned a grisly profit from exhuming newly-buried corpses. She begged Robert to keep watch over her grave and keep it secure. This he promised to do. All through the winter he kept vigil beside the grave and took little note of anything else but this task. When the spring came, Robert assembled his few possessions and gave them away. He walked down to the river, took out his small boat from the reeds and rowed out along the channel. His upturned boat was found a few days later but Robert was never seen again.

Bures

Many were the cunning traps laid to deal with Nazi invaders during the last war. I remember seeing concrete pill-boxes camouflaged as newspaper kiosks and tobacconists' shops. At Bures a pill-box was built actually inside an existing shop-front at what was seen to be a strategic point. The painted wooden fascia that covered the concrete could be dropped on hinges at a moment's notice. Within the defence post was an anti-tank gun already trained on the bridge opposite that spanned the river Stour. That gun would have blasted any invaders off the bridge and into the water. Unfortunately, such war excitements can become embarrassments in times of peace and the solid concrete emplacement stood awkward and unwanted for some thirty years before it was finally cleared and the shop returned to its original purpose.

The same bridge spans the border between Suffolk and Essex, Bures being practically the southernmost point of the county. It is a place predominantly of Saxon history. Somewhere nearby – the exact spot is a matter of debate – the young king Edmund was crowned on December 25th 855 AD. About a mile north-west of Bures is a building called St. Stephens Chapel which is generally believed to mark the place because it was built by Abbot Sampson of Bury St. Edmunds in the 13th century and given over to relics and memorabilia of King Edmund. Each year on November 20th, the complete range of objects was put on show and thousands of pilgrims visited the chapel to pay homage to the saint and martyr, the dead king of the East Angles.

At Smallbridge Hall, for long the residence of the Waldegrave family, Queen Elizabeth I was once entertained – at an unexpected expense, it seems, for the detailed items that made up the total of £250 were listed and later given to the British Museum. John de Waldegrave was Sheriff of London in the 12th century while a kind of record was achieved by a later Waldegrave, Sir Richard, who became Speaker in 1382 and later offered his resignation, the only Speaker ever to do so. It was probably only a gesture anyway – the king quite properly refused to accept it.

Such events make history, no doubt, but it is at a lower level that we find the human interest. In this case it comes from the diary of a kind of peripatetic Excise man of the 18th century, a man who walked the villages hereabouts while engaged in the delicate but necessary task of enforcing the laws on brewing. In those days there were many dodges used by small brewers to defeat the laws, one of them being the widely known Dot-and-Go system. In this, the brewer duly wetted his allotted amount of barley for malting under the official eye of the Excise man, then wetted a second amount as soon as the coast was clear, thus doubling his supply of malt.

This particular officer seems to have been easy-going in the extreme for he speaks often of playing cards and feeling 'fuddled' from drink. When, at Ipswich in August 1786, he was ordered to go to Bures, he secured the high sum of six shillings for expenses and took four days on the journey. 'Dined at Lavenham,' he wrote, 'set out for Bures at one o'clock, got there at five.' (All his journeys were apparently made on foot). 'Found the Officer and wife very smart people like them much don't vastly like my quarters.'

It was not often that he held a good opinion of his colleagues. In September while still at Bures, he wrote: 'the supervisor came – don't half think he slighted me but don't care for him a rainy day hope he will get wet to the skin.'

His lodgings were far from being havens of rest for on different occasions he complains – 'house full almost crazy' and 'up all night could not go to bed for company.' And a week or two later – 'up all Night owing to Hop Pickers taking up the House.' Convivialty cost him a sore head on frequent occasions. 'Got fuddled,' he wrote in his diary, 'felt quite ill all Day.'

Butley

The abbey at Butley was the most important in the county apart from the mother abbey at Bury St. Edmunds. This priory of Augustinian canons was founded in 1171 by Ranulph de Glanville, who became Chief Justice of England. It was generously endowed by de Glanville during the period of his public success but the time came when he fell into disfavour and was removed from office. All his properties were given to his daughters, with the manor of Benhall and the patronage of Butley Abbey to the eldest. Having settled this, he then expressed his extreme mortification at his situation by going to fight in the Holy Wars. At the siege of Acre he fought beside the king, Richard I and showed his mettle as a warrior.

At the Dissolution of the Monasteries, Henry VIII disposed of the abbey to the Duke of Norfolk. In later times it became the property of Mr. George Wright, who constructed the very handsome gate-house using patterns of flint interspersed with Caen stone to pick out the detail of several coats of arms. In a church within the priory grounds was interred the body of Michael de la Pole, Earl of Suffolk, who was killed at Agincourt.

The magnificent approach road to the abbey was planted by monks with groups of beeches along each side. They seem to have been pollarded or stunted in some way unnatural to beeches and instead of towering in their usual majesty, the trees stand now in a grotesque series of witch-like huddles that could belong to some tale by the brothers Grimm.

Butley stands on the edge of Suffolk's forest area, with one foot, so to speak, in woodland and bracken, the other on light agricul-tural land. Nearby are the Forestry Commission's soft-wood plant-ations screened by some of the more traditional of our trees. There are also some very ancient woods hereabouts, with hollies in particular estimated to be a thousand years old. Just as old, in fact, as the small Norman windows still discernible in the dignified and well cared-for parish church, the chancel of which was completed in the 14th century.

In spring the church is bedecked with daffodils, for here are the well-known daffodil woods. Every year since I can remember people have been allowed to go to the woods and collect a handful. When we were young we used to ride there on our cycles on the prescribed Sundays. With the sun shining through the trees on that carpet of gold, it was an excursion that held the very savour of spring.

Buxhall ✑

Of the four ancient manors of Buxhall, the most prominent was that long held by the Coppingers. It was a name that became venerated and later ridiculed in places far removed from the village. It was venerated when Sir William Coppinger, born here in 1512, achieved his long and hard-fought ambition to become Lord Mayor of

London. This was a Dick Whittington story indeed for it required persistence and pluck for a country-bred lad to reach such eminence. It is believed that he filled the office with honour and came back to Buxhall eventually as a man of stature in the countryside. In fact, there is very little more information about Sir William until the making of his will, in which he left half of his wealth to charities and the other half to relations. No doubt all the beneficiaries were duly grateful but one may hope that the charities spent their windfall a little more prudently than the assortment of Coppingers who entered upon a spree of huge proportions, mainly directed to feasting and drinking. 'To live like the Coppingers' became an accepted simile that did nothing to enhance the family reputation.

One of the Coppingers, Walter, was convinced that his health would be in peril if he ever took off his hat. He was so concerned about it that he managed to persuade the king, Henry VIII, to give him a special dispensation from wearing a hat in the royal presence. The actual document, in language quaint to our ears but clear enough in meaning, is kept in the British Museum. It runs:

> 'We be credibly informed that our trusty and well-beloved subject, Walter Coppinger, is so diseased in his head that without his great danger he cannot be conveniently discovered of the same. In consideration thereof we have by these presents licensed him to use and wear his bonet upon his head as well in our presence as elsewhere.'

Campsea Ash 🦢

This scattered village enjoys a history of remarkable variations in its name, which is rooted in Saxon times and carries the association of the once-revered ash tree. Nowadays the favoured spelling is Campsea Ash or Campsea Ashe. On a 1913 postmark it was Campsey Ash, while the Suffolk historian Raven is satisfied to call it Campsey. In earlier days it was Ashe-by-Campsea, Ashe-juxta-Campessey, Camshee Ashe, Ayssch-juxta-Camsey and Capsea Ash.

The river Deben provides a meandering border-line to the west of the village though recently both river and village have been riven by the broad new road that by-passes Wickham Market. Apart from this intrusion and the frequent sorties in the air from the nearby U.S.

base at Bentwaters, everything looks peaceful enough. Within these boundaries is the unexpected importance of a railway station boldly stated to be Wickham Market Station. Unsuspecting travellers who have come this way by train in the idle belief that Wickham Market station would be a station at Wickham Market have felt less than enchanted to find themselves at least two miles away from that town and deposited on a country road near nowhere in particular.

There was once a nunnery here, founded by Matilda of Lancaster, descendant of Edmund Crouchback, brother of Edward I. She entered the nunnery herself with eighteen women of the order but later changed her religious allegiance.

The most prominent son of Campsea Ash was undoubtedly Viscount Ullswater, known hereabouts as a great landowner and farmer but in more sophisticated circles as a leading statesman, serving as Speaker of the House of Commons from 1905 to 1921 and in many another exalted position far removed from the fields of Ashe-by-Campsea.

Cavendish

If a county can have a 'better half', then I am sure the area that used to be designated as West Suffolk must be it. It holds all the prestigious and rather precious villages including Clare, Cavendish, Lavenham, Chelsworth — the very names themselves seeming to belong to a geographical *Debrett*.

Perhaps this is appropriate enough, particularly in the case of Cavendish, since the family that took this name for their own now upstages most of the peerage with a dukedom. It was the Gernons, a well-known and ambitious family with a seat here at Cavendish, who felt that they had practically everything except a good resounding name. Accordingly, they became the Cavendishes of Cavendish and forthwith impressed themselves as well as everyone else with their style. Distinguished as the Gernons had never been, they were soon rewarded with honours. John Cavendish, now a knight, was appointed Chief Justice of the King's Bench in the turbulent 14th century and served his king with zeal.

Sir John's undoing came with the Peasants' Revolt of 1381 and was caused by the unwitting action of his own son. It was a time of total unrest in the countryside and Suffolk rebels joined the revolt

CAVENDISH

against old and unfair conditions of service. At Smithfield, as the history books tell us, the young king Richard II met the mob led by Wat Tyler, who made as if to draw his sword and was mortally wounded by a dagger thrust wielded by the Lord Mayor of London. Also by the king's side was John Cavendish, the Chief Justice's youngest son who, as esquire to the king felt it his duty to despatch the rebel leader finally with his sword. His action brought the reward of an immediate honour for himself but a tragic end to his father. In Suffolk, the rebels furiously attacked and ransacked the home of the Chief Justice before dragging him off to Bury St. Edmunds. There he was summarily beheaded and his head placed on the pillory in the market place.

Such violence does not fit well with this most peaceful of villages. The whole atmosphere here, with the large green fringed with picturesque houses, is that of comfortable placidity. In fact, if there is a fault to be found at all with Cavendish, it is in its rather self-conscious perfection. It gives me the impression that some dire punishment and even torture could await some unthinking stranger who dropped a toffee-paper on to this well-kept sward. It goes without saying that Cavendish has several times won the Best Kept Village competition and is a little put out when it does not.

Just opposite the green is the house called the Old Rectory. Those who do not recognise the name will know the name of its principal occupant, Sue Ryder. Principal occupant because here in her own house she provides an international sanctuary for some of the deprived and dispossessed of the world.

Craftsmen of three centuries contributed to the building of the church of St. Mary, which contains a variety of treasures. Among them is a brass lectern said to have been presented by Queen Elizabeth I and a most elaborately-carved chest of the 14th century.

Chelsworth 🐚

It is now accepted as Chelsworth though given in White's Suffolk of 1844 as Chellesworth. This peaceful village with its half-timbered houses and placid open spaces is situated in the valley of the Brett where two small tributaries come together about five miles north of Hadleigh. Close by the church are the ruins of a very large mansion believed to have been the home of some very eminent person. The fields around are called the Park or Park Fields.

The painstaking work of an artistic monk from the medieval Abbey of St. Edmund was discovered in the church about the middle of the last century and caused a local sensation. It was while some restoration work was being carried out on the chancel walls that a remarkable Doom painting was suddenly revealed. In the clearest detail it showed Christ on a rainbow with cherubs and angels in attendance but confronted by the figure of Satan, complete with horns and barbed tail and with flames all around.

Like most villages, Chelsworth has its memorial to the dead of the Great War, all the more admirable, perhaps in that only one young man failed to return.

'The people of Chelsworth erected this tablet in proud memory of Charles Peck, who gave his life for his country in the Great War, 25th September, 1917, aged 19.'

Clare ✣

Like its near neighbour, Cavendish, Clare sits with some dignity beside the Stour and just so much removed from the Essex border. A thousand years and more of history have bestowed upon Clare a visible legacy from every separate age and created a kind of aura derived from the whole. It is not the ruined castle alone or the church or priory, nor the names and tombs of the famous that strike the visitor so much as the general atmosphere in which all these constituents seem to have been ingested long ago.

The stranger, however, has to view the parts separately and could not do better than to begin with the castle. Not that there is a castle with any kind of entity but enough tell-tale signs litter the site to fire the imagination. For one thing it was of prodigious size and strength, with all the features associated with a Norman castle though it was built long before the Conqueror was born, probably during the Saxon heptarchy. It seems a remarkable fortress for the East Angles to find necessary in that area, for it covered some twenty acres, with an outer and inner bailey surrounded by a moat and a wall. The keep stood magnificently upon the top of a mound at least sixty feet high. Now the mound survives but little else.

With the coming of William I, Clare was made one of the 95 lordships in the county and it was given by the king to a relation, Richard Fitz Gilbert, for his aid at the battle of Hastings. The castle then became the baronial seat of the Earls of Clare. Unfortunately, the line only continued for three of four generations before coming to a natural end without male issue. The estate was divided between three sisters, one of them Elizabeth, sometimes called the Lady of Clare. It was she who endowed and refounded the second oldest Cambridge college and called it Clare.

Close to the castle was the priory, founded in 1248 and occupied as a monastery of Augustinian canons. It was later given by Henry VIII to Richard Friend who transformed the building into a dwelling for himself. The priory church was used thenceforward as a barn although it covered the body of Joan of Acres, second daughter of Edward I and his queen Eleanor, who was married to the ninth Earl of Clare.

The church of St. Peter and St. Paul has been well endowed and beautified through succeeding generations after its original building in the 13th century. From the majestic appearance of the church it is believed that it was erected by the lordly Clares and only later on permission was given for commoners to use it. The original walls of the tower are four feet thick. The nave was extended in the 15th century, the chancel altered in the 17th century and considerable changes were made in the last century between 1834 and 1836, part of the work being the extending of seating capacity by building a gallery. The result is this church of today that looks as proud as it is beautiful.

Claydon ✥

Perhaps Claydon was always too well-placed for its own good. Even when a distance of four miles from the county town gave it some immunity from the urban spreading sickness, it was in the path of what transport that existed. The turnpikes that brought horse-drawn traffic from Bury St. Edmunds and from Norwich joined together here in the centre of the village. Barges came up the Gipping to take lime and whiting from the factory and was joined by the railway when cement became the local industry.

No wonder that Claydon is now a focal point for roads going north and west from Ipswich and Felixstowe. A great roundabout with flyover now distributes fast-moving traffic to all points of the compass, while the old village hangs on in some stubborn loyalty to the past. Close by the roundabout is the lane leading to the old water-mill that once made paper and afterwards took to grinding corn. There were many small cottages here and footpaths through meadows to the river. Where the roundabout now stands was an area of wet meadowland that for generations carried nothing more than osiers and masses of rosebay willow-herb. The road men turned the river away, dug out thousands of tons of bog and replaced it with sand then demolished many of the cottages in the lane and banished the life-long tenants from their familiar haunts. A few of the cottagers, in varying degrees of distress, went to live in the vast housing estate on the Barham side of the village where once Kirby meandered in 18th century peace.

Two coaching inns stand in the old centre of the village where a lane rises quite steeply to the 15th century church and to the farmhouse on the site of a moated castle. High on another hill, the

45

centuries-old eyes of Mockbeggar Hall look down on lines of traffic passing through what was once its own private estate.

Cockfield

Surely there was never another village with so many Greens about it. Eastward of the Sudbury to Bury St. Edmunds road, which at this point includes a good stretch of Roman origin, there is Oldhall Green, Cross Green, Great Green, Colchester Green, Thorpe Green, Almshouse Green, Buttons Green, Smithwood Green and Windsor. Together, they almost encircle the village.

Did Robert Louis Stevenson know all these Greens? Almost certainly he did. He knew and loved Cockfield and lived to be grateful to it for it was here that he found the encouragement for his literary career. Under the aegis of the vicar, Churchill Babington, who was a distinguished scholar and writer, R.L.S. met Sidney

STUBBLE FIELD
GREAT GREEN
COCKFIELD

Colvin, – a meeting that seemed to put a seal on both their careers. Colvin put the young writer on the road to success with practical help and advice as well as sincere faith in his ability and later in life was to complete his interest in R.L.S. by writing his biography.

There may be little here now that tells of Stevenson's visits but one can share the pleasure he must have had in this scattered, friendly village consisting of two ancient manors. One was Cockfield Hall which originally belonged to the Abbey of St. Edmunds and was given to Sir William Spring after the Dissolution. The other, Earls Hall, was so named because it was owned by the Earls of Oxford. The estate was forfeited at one time because one of the Oxfords chose the wrong side in the Wars of the Roses but it was later restored.

This is in the heart of farming country. While the shade of R.L.S. may give us only a flimsy pretext for coming here, the charm and situation of the place confirms it as a good enough reason.

Coddenham ✺

It was a hundred and fifty years ago when Kirby, the naturalist, declared that the Spanish chestnut trees of Coddenham were the best to be seen in the whole county. Perhaps they are still. These majestic trees that grace the park that Nicholas Bacon devised provide oases of shade in the summer and successfully hide the Hall from the passer-by. Unfortunately, the magnificent horse-chestnuts that used to stand close beside the road and almost shadowing the church across the way, have not fared so well and are now sadly diminished.

Nathaniel Bacon, the Cromwellian statesman, lived here close by the family's seat at Shrubland Park. Less well-remembered of this vast and distinguished family was Nicholas – who built the Hall and planted the chestnuts – and Philip, who fought gallantly in the sea battle against the Dutch off the Suffolk coast and later died a hero's death.

In Roman times the village was an important administration and transport centre. They built a fort beside where now the hump backed bridge straddles the soggy ditch of the river Gipping and they contrived to leave enough of their goods and chattels behind to inspire many an enthusiastic archeological 'dig'. Perhaps the most rewarding of these was a 2000 year old kiln which was unearthed in such perfect condition that it was fired again forthwith with complete success.

Since the beginning of the century, the fortunes of the village have declined. A charming medley of picturesque cottages now house no more than 500 souls and many of these, of course, strangers. The decline in numbers has robbed the natives of shops and services formerly enjoyed, including the popular Crown Inn. The old forge still exists as a recognisable shell that tells us little of the days when there would be as many as ten horses waiting there to be shod.

Determined to see the famed alabaster carving in the church, I was a little taken aback to find it no more than a small framed artefact of about 18 inches by 12 inches. It depicts a crucifixion with angels holding chalices for the blood. The carving is almost priceless, I am told.

There was great excitement at one time at the discovery of some tunnels in the grounds of the old rectory, one of them over one hundred feet long. Sober consideration, however, brought the conclusion that the tunnels had merely been drains to a soakaway.

Cookley ✺

This is one of those villages that seem to vanish before your eyes and you have to seek the church in order to establish some focal point. There is some reward for doing so for here there is a fine Norman archway (though what was once a doorway beneath is now blocked up) and inside, a host of carvings on pews and choir stalls. The dark timber of the hammer-beam roof looks pleasingly mellow as if from the centuries' long devotions below. William and Margery Browne are remembered on a brass on the wall, the couple shown in Elizabethan costume and with the figures of eight small children by their side.

Cookley has another Tudor associaton, for it was part of a gift of recompense for Anne of Cleves when Henry VIII found that she was not at all the sort of bride he had hoped for and wanted to get rid of her.

There is no feeling of isolation among the local people. It is accepted as outright farming country and quite happy to be a satellite of the town of Halesworth, only two or three miles to the north. Here are all the basic but adequate needs of the rural communities.

Covehithe 🦢

It looks strange and stark against the immense skyline of the Suffolk coast. Tall, jagged arches and tumbling walls sprout upwards in the ruins of an enormous medieval church and among the fallen masonry another tower of a later church, as if it were an abortive off-shoot of the other, joins the scene of desolation. It seems a rather dark and forbidding legacy for such a small, unassuming village that shelters only half a mile from the sea. The forsaken tower looks all the more forlorn because of the faces and figures on walls and battlements, angels and grotesques together looking down as if reflecting on the futility of human effort.

Bilious Bale lived here when he was not following his argumentative path to power in the Church. John Bale — named 'Bilious' because of his ranting and nagging manner of speech — graduated from the Carmelite College at Norwich to go on to Oxford but came to the notice of Thomas Cromwell and under his patronage renounced for a time his career in the church in order to write morality plays. When Cromwell fell from favour, he himself felt it prudent to exile himself to Germany and like so many others became involved in the see-saw of Tudor religion. Returning to England on the accession of the young king Edward VI he was fully recompensed for his exile by being made a bishop but at the king's untimely death had to escape again from the vengeful clutches of Mary Tudor. It was not until Elizabeth followed her sister to the throne that he dared return, still inveighing against the tyranny of enforced religion but thankful to retire to the peace of the countryside.

The Creetings 🦢

The Creetings have been chopped up rather mercilessly in recent years by new roads and it takes a little imagination to remember that in days of more static village life, there were three separate little hamlets here. They were situated close together in an odd little backwater near Needham Market, each of them with a church, two of the churches so close together the community became known as Creeting Two-Churches. The hamlet of St. Olave's was ever the tiniest of the three but its church was still standing in 1532 when John Pinkeney ordered that he should be buried in the chancel. In the following century the church began to crumble and soon disappeared.

All Saint's church survived for somewhat longer but eventually became ruinous and was taken down. It was then discovered that there were no foundations and that the church had simply been erected on levelled ground. Except for Creeting St. Peter, the church of St. Mary's now serves the whole community.

Creeting St. Mary was established in medieval days as a Priory and formed a cell of a Normandy abbey until the influence of foreign religious houses was suppressed. It was then made over to Eton College, the Provost and Fellows of which are still lords of the manor.

Creeting St. Peter is sometimes called West Creeting. The 14th century church stands rather remotely on a hill surrounded by trees. Nearby is Bosmere Hall, a mansion whose local fame is represented by its lake. Local superstition claims that the lake – the Mere – is bottomless. It seems a strange conviction to last into this scientific age and may originate in the efforts of parents to keep their children in some awe of its dangers.

Culford

In a great 500 acre park here beside the river Lark, are gathered the church, the rectory and the magnificent Hall. The Hall was built by Sir Nicholas Bacon, step-brother of Francis of the history books and later handed down to his seventh son, Nathaniel. Monuments in the church revere particularly this member of the Bacon family and recall him as an artist and a botanist. His wife has the unusual distinction of receiving posthumous praise for having rescued two impoverished families by marrying into them.

The most distinguished occupant of the Hall was the Marquis of Cornwallis, to whom it passed through marriage. He had vast reconstruction work put in hand and doubtless looked forward to peaceful years at Culford. Unfortunately, it was not to be. Public commitments and private tragedy robbed him of the solace he hoped for. Even as an old man he was called forth again to become Governor General of India but died there soon after his arrival.

Altogether he had no more than three clear years at Culford and these were clouded by family deaths. In one week in 1655 he lost a small son and a daughter, and in all four children were taken from him in their infancy. His feeling of guilt at the defeat at Yorktown of the forces under his command added to his unhappiness. In truth his heart had never been in the war against the colonists who seemed so much like his own people.

The present church was built in the 19th century by Sir Stephen Fox, whose daughter was married to the third Lord Cornwallis. Besides monuments to the Bacon family it carries a magnificent marble tomb of Beatrix Craven, Countess Cadogan, who died here in 1907.

Dalham 🐝

The Kennet is no more than a rivulet here and wooden footbridges cross it at intervals in the charming village street. Famous men have walked here and two of them were of the name of Rhodes. Of the two brothers, the one that matters most hereabouts is not he who helped to found an Empire in Africa but his greatest ally and admirer, Francis, as great a patriot as Cecil and perhaps a greater man. Both lived here for a time since their grandfather owned the Hall and its estate but both followed their roving spirits and spent their adventurous destinies in Africa. It was Francis who acknowledged his deep roots in his native village and though he died in Africa only a short distance from where his famous brother already lay, he was brought back to the place he loved. He was only 54. Most of those years were spent in Africa as a loyal soldier, for he was present at Khartoum, at Ladysmith, took part in the Jameson Raid and was in the van of those who relieved Mafeking. At one time he was taken prisoner by the Boers and sentenced to death. After the war, still fascinated by Africa, he set out to explore and record the country from the Cape to the Zambesi but died before he could complete his self-imposed mission.

In Dalham, Francis had restored the church roof as a memorial to his brother and in turn a memorial was set up to recall the life of this outstanding man:

'Long travel in this churchyard ends
A gentleman who knew not fear,
A soldier, sportsman, prince of friends,
A man men could but love, lies here.'

Startling events are rare in Dalham and perhaps that is why the ancient affair of Oliver Cromwell and the church spire is still brought up in local gossip. Both came to a sudden end on the same day and the fact is recounted as if there was some moral or portent to be found in it. If there is one, it escapes me.

Darsham

For most of us who travel along the A12, the name of Darsham means one thing – a level crossing and a substantial but rather lonely-looking hotel at the side. This is the Stradbroke Arms and so far as the hasty traveller can see, the complete Darsham. It is something of a surprise and certainly a kind of reward for the effort, to find the very real village tucked away at the side. There is a scattered community of houses, many of them old-style with thatched roofs, in a pleasant association with the ancient church of All Saints. Unassuming enough in appearance, All Saints could nevertheless boast a seniority over others if it chose to do so since parts of an original Norman church are incorporated in the building. Nearby is Brussels Green, once a common on which local cottagers were able to graze their animals, but is now enclosed.

It is no uncommon thing for those who build or repair large houses or churches and are proud of their work, to put a signature somewhere concealed until such time as later workmen may be required again. A few years ago the names of a carpenter and his mate were found in a window-frame of the Stradbroke Arms, pencilled signatures that have survived within the woodwork for over a century. On April 27th 1859, the two men A. Malting and J. Baker bid for a kind of posterity and certainly succeeded.

During the same modernisation work it was found that the cellars had lenghts of rail track for cross beams. No doubt the rails are part of the old line of the Southwold to Halesworth railway, which probably very few people can remember as it closed in 1929. There was something fabulous and completely comic about the Great Little Railway and produced in passengers a feeling of enjoyment rather than irritation. A whole series of comic postcards of the railway remain as a reminder. Some show passengers getting off the train to pick flowers and the engine driver making tea, while on the platform old folk with long beards and covered with cob-webs from their long wait, survey the train with unbelieving eyes. Although I never travelled on the train, I remember the postcards and the jokes very clearly. In the twenties there was always time to spare. I doubt if present-day rail travel in Suffolk could raise the same kind of a smile.

Dennington

'The reason why I decided to come with you today,' said my least favourite nephew, who knows everything, 'is because of the pyx.'

We were entering the porch of Dennington's magnificent church. 'Picks? Pics?' I asked, scratching my memory. For a stupid moment I thought it was a contraction of 'pictures'.

'Obviously,' said my nephew in his best know-all voice, 'I shall have to tell you what a pyx is. It is the ancient keeping place of the vessels of the Sacrament. This pyx is almost unique.'

It is certainly a rare find in a church. This cone-shaped cover was made in the 15th century and coloured red, green and gold. It hovers above the altar like a gigantic candle-snuffer. But my curiosity soon led me away to gaze at other treasures. For there is a wealth of ancient objects in the church and a wealth of background colour and ornamentation to set them off. Strange to think that at the end of the last war the church was in danger of becoming a ruin. Years of neglect, of village pennies going to help buy a Spitfire instead of into the offertory box, brought calls for action when peace-time conditions returned. A massive restoration plan was put into effect and the church stands now as rich and as proud as it ever was, unashamedly waiting to be visited and wondered at.

It would be a mistake to try and mention everything to be found in the interior since it would sound like a mere catalogue of objects which need to be seen as part of the whole. I remember in particular the elaborate carving in both wood and stone, in screens and in figures, on bench ends and roof beams. There is a long sand table on which children once learned to shape their letters, an ancient bier and an enormous chest, seven feet long, that stands in the vestry. Unusual, too, the Jacobean pulpit that is trebly useful, being not only pulpit but reading desk and clerk's desk all in one.

The shield and picture of the eminent churchman, Dean Colet, can be seen within. He was a son of the Sir Henry Colet who twice became Lord Mayor of London. Dean Colet took up the benefice here as a young man of nineteen and in due course became Dean of St. Paul's and the founder of St. Paul's School. It is of some interest that he was one of eleven sons and eleven daughters.

Reposing in alabaster effigies are the figures of Lord Bardolph and his wife. This was the redoubtable Sir William Phelip, soldier and courtier and he reclines here in the armour that he had worn in battle. His peerage came from his marriage to the heiress of the Bardolph title and fortune and for this reason his wife lies in alabaster splendour on his right side instead of his left, as was usual. Lord Bardolph had provided for their immortal souls in the manner of the time by founding a chantry in a separate chapel of the church. Here, two priests were charged with the duty of offering prayers daily for the couple, in life and in death.

This is no shrinking violet of a church, lost among trees or in solitude down a side lane. It stands impressively within and yet somewhat above the community around – houses, school, post office, shop and pub all closely gathered in. Just here the roads from many directions come together almost under the ancient walls and the tower seems to look down benignly on all who pass by.

Denston 🐦

In 1944, as the Allies pushed the Germans back from the Channel coast and the prospect of victory brought dreams of a rose-hued peace, villages like Denston were beginning to formulate plans for the future. What had necessarily been left undone by the requirements of war must now be done to restore and enhance the life of the village. Those who were left to carry the parish flag at Denston decided that when peace came they could do no less than build a hall, such a fine recreation and memorial hall as they had never had before.

The plan simmered for many years, with other priorities constantly coming forward but the fact that it was not until 1960 that
the hall was finished indicates an unending devotion to the purpose
rather than otherwise. Every year collections from whist drives,
competitions and jumble sales mounted up until they reached the
magic figure of one thousand pounds. With a grant from the
Ministry of Education it would be enough provided they built the
hall themselves. So, for three years the people of Denston, of every
age from six years old to eighty, worked on the project. In
November 1960, fifteen years after the war had finished, the
splendid new hall was officially opened. At the ceremony the six
leaders of the project were presented with the freedom of the hall.

Denston (or Denardeston) still has the homely, old-world atmosphere in which one can believe in the success of such community
projects, while those on a larger scale suffer all the slings and arrows
of modern cynicism and self-interest. The village lies some six miles
north of Clare and has a spacious, park-like appearance particularly
around the Hall. There is some evidence that Denston Hall was once
a fortified dwelling with a moat.

For those who admire the delicate skills of the wood carver, there
is much to be discovered in the church. It seems that wherever you
look there is ancient timber which has been beautified by craftsmen,
from the Jacobean font to the roof beams and especially in the
chancel screens. A fascinating variety of creatures pose on the bench
ends to make the visitor pause and share in the joy that must have
gone into their making.

One day in 1948 a farmyard turkey took a fancy to the church
and its open door and forthwith laid an egg on the velvet cover of
the communion table. Things ecclesiastic seemed to attract this
wandering fowl for it had already hatched a clutch of young poults
on a tombstone.

It is unlikely that either this event or the building of the village hall
will figure very large in world affairs but nevertheless they are the
stuff of which village life is made.

Dunwich

The merchants, shipowners and traders of the busy port of Dunwich must have known the earth was shifting beneath their feet even at the time of its greatest prosperity. A thousand years ago the coastline was gradually disappearing. Edward the Confessor had included a spit of land here in his tax survey that the compilers of the Domesday Book searched for in vain. Erosion has been slow but insistent. The rich people who once lived and made their fortunes here could ignore the warnings for they were never urgent and no one was likely to get his feet wet in his own lifetime. And after all, it was the sea and this splendid port that provided Dunwich with its commercial wealth. Records of the reign of Edward I give some conception of the size of the port with a list of shipping that included 11 ships of war, 16 'fair' ships, 20 barks trading to Scandinavia and 24 fishing boats plying along the coast. In 1359 Dunwich had sent 6 warships and 102 men to assist at the siege of Calais while Orford sent only half as many.

Perhaps the greatest achievement of this enterprising town was the provision, at its own expense and by its own workmen, of 11 ships of war for use against the French, each vessel fully equipped and with a complement of 72 men. But even then the sea was battering at the town and in the aftermath of storms the devastation

DUNWICH
SUFFOLK

was immense. In the middle of the 14th century a substantial part of Dunwich, including 400 houses, was lost. Soon after, the churches of St. Leonard, St. Martin and St. Nicholas also disappeared. Two hundred years later the port was destroyed, the church of St. John Baptist taken down and St. Catherine had crumbled over the cliffs together with the chapels of St. Francis and St. Anthony. By 1715 the sea had reached the old market place, gathered the town hall, the gaol and all else in its path into its ever-hungry vastness and left no more than the memory of the town's greatness. St. Peter's church fell next and provided the local people with a particularly harrowing spectacle. As the churchyard was washed away the skeletons of those long buried could be seen in the sand below the cliffs.

In the present century it has been the turn of All Saints, the last church of all, to disappear. In 1900 the tower of the church was tottering on the edge and by 1904 part of the chancel had fallen. Two years later the nave had gone and by the outbreak of the Great War only a piece of the tower and one arch remained. A single stubborn buttress rested there until 1919 when it was dragged away and later set up as a memorial to the lost town.

Earl Soham

I am afraid I spent quite a large part of my ignorant youth wondering what a shimmaker was. Nowadays there is no need to know. The shoemaker has gone with all the other tradesmen that somehow earned a living within a small community. In Earl Soham, admittedly a large village, there were five shimmakers at work half way through the last century. In addition there were these:

A thatcher	A bricklayer
A malster	Two blacksmiths
A brickmaker	Two wood turners
A saddler	Two wheelwrights
A watchmaker	Two tailors
A glover	Five carpenters
A whip maker who was also a hairdresser	

On the other side of the counter there were few great spenders in the community. Two clergymen, two school teachers, a handful of independent gentlemen, a dozen farmers and an untold number of farm labourers seems few indeed to keep so many craftsmen busy.

Among all these varied occupations it is still something of a surprise to hear of a sea-captain in the village's past history. He was Robert Wyard, a generous benefactor apparently through his relief and gratitude at having survived a shipwreck. His will directed that each year a sermon should be delivered by the rector in his name and alms distributed – but after the sermon and not before.

The church has a fine setting at one end of the long main street and close to the old rectory and a cluster of substantial houses. Inside the church there is the warm welcome of polished wood and a cared-for atmosphere. Both chancel and nave reveal a wealth of carved figures of such an independent variety it seems that craftsmen indulged their own tastes and skills in deciding upon their subject. Here are creatures of all kinds from a fish to an elephant and one or two human figures apparently engaged in the harvest, while fantasy creeps in with such ideas as a camel with two heads.

With some reason, past rectors have lived out long lives here, serving this beautiful church and the village. In the 17th century Francis Folkes was rector for 54 years but this was exceeded later on by Francis Capper who stayed for 59 years. Richard Abbay made a comparatively hurried visit of only 48 years.

East Bergholt ✒

This is a large and prestigious village only a mile or so from the main London road south-west of Ipswich and not much further from the broadening estuary of the Stour. It is generally regarded as John Constable's village and there is an atmosphere here still, despite the flocks of tourists and trippers, which can persuade one that there was something special here to inspire the painter.

Certainly he loved the place where he was born and his childhood was no doubt formative of the artistic eye. He would have been fascinated by the line and colour of old houses, of the beautiful church and the strange bell-tower in the churchyard. But most of all that was significant to the artist was the rural scene about Flatford Mill, just two miles away, with the broad sky and the calm fields of the Vale of Dedham. Much of the essential quality of this area has been preserved into our modern lives despite vast difficulties arising from the constant invasions by interested people.

The church here in which Constable worshipped is a large and magnificent structure, forty yards long it is said and with forty windows. The exterior is of flint and stone with an impressive show of battlements and turrets. The parapets above the walls are lined with shields and there is distinction in the lines of column and buttress about the ancient building. There were three centuries in the making of it from the beginning in the 14th century. Inside, many of the fine furnishings have been contributed by well-to-do worshippers here. Notably, a screen to the lady chapel was given in memory of 80 years of singing in the choir. In this way, Mr. Mann showed his gratitude for a long life of singing and also for a happy marriage since he added a screen to the chancel for a memento of this. The lectern too, is in thanksgiving for 40 years of married life enjoyed by another parishioner.

John Constable had his share of good and bad fortune but it was smiling on him on that day that he met little Maria Bicknell in the church. She was the rector's grand-daughter and only twelve years old but there was immediate sympathy between the two and they waited patiently for the day when they could marry. In this, John was doubly blessed – with Maria herself and with her considerable fortune which allowed him to see his artistic future clear ahead without monetary doubts and fears.

Perhaps the most unusual feature in the village is the wooden structure within the churchyard. It is a bell-cage, a building with an open lattice of beams in which are housed five great bells. They weigh over four tons and are rung by hand. They have remained in this odd bell-cage for 400 years, since they were put there temporarily, it was believed, while the tower was being completed.

Among the memorials to distinguished past-parishioners is one on the interior wall of the church to a schoolmaster. He gave of his best for eleven years but was then 'unfortunately shot'. It is an intriguing statement that yields no further explanation.

John Constable left East Bergholt for London when he was 23 years old and found that there was no sudden acclaim for his work.

On the contrary, he spent many years of disappointment, occupying himself mainly in copying. He was 43 when he exhibited *The White Horse* at the Royal Academy and a few years older before recognition came, not from his own countrymen but from Paris, where *The Hay Wain* aroused intense admiration and incited French artists to imitate.

Easton

Everybody loves a crinkle-crankle wall. I don't know why but a straight wall is just a wall, while a crinkle-crankle wall is a joy forever. Its loveliness increases. One of the best and most undulating of such walls is here at Easton, where it surrounds the estate of Easton Park. The man who built the wall and the mansion it encloses was Anthony Wingfield, created a baronet in 1607 though not entirely because of the wall. The estate then passed to the Earls of Rochford until that line came to an end. It was taken over by the Duke of Hamilton who rarely graced the village with his presence, having vast estates also in Scotland.

There are Wingfield brasses in the church of All Saints, paying tribute to the Elizabethan John Wingfield and huge box pews with the Wingfield arms carved on them. The 14th century church stands close to the village centre and has a square tower that becomes octagonal at the top.

The most notable of the less exalted families of Easton was Thomas Short. Against all sorts of difficulties he became a doctor in London at the time of the Restoration and lived to be hailed as a genius by some of his colleagues. Unfortunately, Thomas was a Catholic at an inappropriate moment for Catholics and the House of Lords made a great fuss and demanded his expulsion from the College of Physicians. It was to the great credit of that learned College that they refused to do anything of the kind.

Easton has a comfortable, tucked-up sort of atmosphere that is only slightly disturbed nowadays by the many visitors to the Farm Park, where old and new breeds of farm animals are on show to the public. The Earls of Rochford can never have foreseen such a thing happening on their private land.

Elmswell 🌿

The extent and wealth of the Abbey of Bury St. Edmunds in the Middle Ages was enormous. Apart from the cells and priories and colleges all over the county, here at Elmswell was evidence of the style and importance to which the Abbot was accustomed. It was said that the Grange was equipped and furnished in a manner fit for a king and indeed a king, Henry VI, did come to visit the Abbot here in 1433. Magnificent as the mansion was, however, it saw the Abbot only on rare occasions for he had several other country seats.

In that year of the king's visit, the church here was almost completed, having been begun almost a hundred years before. Much love and craftsmanship seems to have gone into the building of it for the patterns and varied colours of the flints and the careful stonework give a distinction to the tower and nave.

In the chancel is a marble tablet recalling the 54 years that Joseph Lawson served as a minister here while alone in splendour in the north chapel is the monument to Sir Robert Gardener, Chief Justice of Ireland in the 16th century. Splendid it deserves to be for he was a generous man and ever concerned for the poor in his native village. Lying here now in scarlet and gold robes lined with ermine, he carries a book of law in one hand and gloves in the other. His son, also richly dressed, kneels at his feet. Sir Robert was 80 when he died, having been a chief justice for 18 years.

He had already erected an almshouse in the village for six poor widows – three from Elmswell, three from Woolpit – and stated his hope that succeeding owners of the manor would keep the buildings in good repair. There was also land to be given to the almspeople with a load of firewood each winter. Other of his legacies were for the unhoused poor of the village.

Elveden 🌿

Just before the traveller from the south reaches the Thetford forest, he comes to the tiny village of Elveden. The busy A11 road passes close by but does not disturb the charm nor give an inkling of the surprise to be found here. For, despite the homely look of the woods and heathland, there is hidden away a touch of the exotic, a hint of another, distant continent. Even the war memorial makes such rustics as myself stop and stare. It is 113 feet high and forms an immense column that is hollow. Inside, there are 148 steps to the top which is surmounted by a great stone urn. The memorial reminds the passer-by of the sadness of war in general and of the men of Elveden, Eriswell and Icklingham in particular who did not return to the peace of Suffolk and their homes.

The magnificent Hall here, enclosed in a park behind ancient trees, discloses another unexpected sight — of a huge copper dome over a part of the building. It is a promise of the stranger features within — strange, that is, in the context of our quiet lives and undramatic countryside. For this was the home of the Maharajah Duleep Singh, an anglophile who retained many of the objects and customs of his own land but endeavoured to combine the best of both. His particular contribution to the house was the creation of what is called the Indian Hall, which is surmounted by that copper dome and supported by 28 columns. There are also huge doors covered by copper which has been richly decorated.

When he died, the Maharajah was buried here close by, leaving the Hall, the new church and the neighbourhood a little enriched by his sojourn here in a strange land.

There had been a church beside the Hall ever since the 14th century but it became ruinous with only the tower and fragments of the original remaining. In the same perimeter a new church was built, larger than the other and possessing a grandeur not usually associated with modern standards. The blue and grey of patterned flints and intermediate stonework look down on cloisters built in 1922 in memory of Lady Iveagh. Inside, there is a floor of black and white marble and an alabaster font — and everywhere there is the delight of exquisite carving and seemly ornamentation.

Erwarton

There is no village so small and unassuming that it cannot reveal some bizarre affairs in its past. At Erwarton, tucked away at the tip of the Shotley peninsula where the Stour and Orwell meet, a legend persists that the church here shelters the heart of a queen. And it is a famous queen, too, no other than the ill-fated Anne Boleyn who figures in this story.

Her association with Erwarton came when her aunt married one of the Calthorpes who held the manor here. The relationship brought Anne to stay in the village both before and after she became queen, apparently much taken by the peace of this quiet corner of the kingdom. When she met her unhappy fate, friends and sympathisers went to the place where her body lay and took the heart, bearing it with all respect to the church at Erwarton. Legend it could well be up to this point because there is no real evidence that this occurred but as recently as 1837 a heart-shaped casket was found in the church during extensive renovations. It contained a handful of dust – perhaps the heart of a queen. Enough credence was given to the story to ensure that the casket was buried again in a vault beneath the organ.

In fact, there is much that is Tudor here at Erwarton. The original 14th century church was reconstructed at that time and there is a flourish of Tudor roses and other ornamentation. Inside the church is a monument to Isabel Davillers, daughter of the earliest known owners of the manor, who as a wealthy heiress brought her fortune as well as her person to her marriage with Sir Robert Bacon, so allowing that illustrious family to continue to live in the style to which it had accustomed itself.

In the Civil War, the village was a gathering place for stern loyalists who, on a notable occasion, fought bravely against a force of Roundheads until their ammunition ran out. With inspired ingenuity they took down the church bells and used the metal to continue the battle. Such are the legends of Erwarton.

Euston

Here, 'where noble Grafton spreads his rich domains' was a place of enchantment for Robert Bloomfield, the Suffolk poet. And no doubt it still seems enchanted to many another who feels the poetry of Euston even if he does not express it. The village green is a picture of rustic simplicity with its neat cottages, the view of the bridge across the Thet rivulet and a glimpse of the Hall in the distance, all within a background of beautiful trees. Wisely, the poet kept his verses to descriptions of the rural scene and did not seem too bothered about such things as inequality of wealth:

'Where noble Grafton spreads his rich domains
Round Euston's watered vale and sloping plains;
Where woods and groves in solemn grandeur rise,
Where the kite brooding unmolested flies;
The woodcock and the painted pheasant race,
And skulking foxes destined for the chase.'

There is still a grandeur here though much of the former parkland now inevitably serves a more useful agricultural purpose. The Hall itself is a majestic building though modern, the old Hall having been burned down in 1902. There was some controversy over whether this was a calamity or a blessing, some claiming that the Hall, built during the reign of Charles II, was very ugly and deserved to be destroyed. The diarist Evelyn, however, considered it to be a 'noble pile'.

It certainly had some memorable stories to tell. Perhaps the most entertaining was that relating to a member of the Rokewood family, occupants of the Hall in Tudor times. The current owner when Elizabeth came to the throne was Edward Rokewood, who happened to be an ardent Catholic and no doubt was much put about when the queen, on her procession through the county, decided to pay him a visit. All signs of his preferred faith were hidden to Edward's own satisfaction but not skilfully enough to hoodwink the astute Elizabeth. After observing certain signs and evidence of religious rites, she searched thoroughly and found an image of the Virgin Mary covered with straw in a loft. It was an unfortunate day for Edward. Elizabeth ordered the figure to be burned and Edward to be escorted straightway to Norwich gaol where he served a period of imprisonment.

First of the Grafton line at Euston Hall was Sir Henry Bennet, who fought for the king in the Civil War and was rewarded with many honours at the Restoration, becoming eventually Viscount Thetford and Earl of Arlington. The king was also happy to bless the union of his own son, Henry Grafton, to the Earl of Arlington's daughter. Henry was nine years old and his bride five at the time of this happy event.

Henry, the first Duke of Grafton, became a valiant and dedicated soldier who fought against Monmouth in the Rebellion, distinguished himself at the Battle of Beachy Head and served with honour beside Marlborough in Ireland. There he was wounded at the storming of Cork and died soon after, not yet thirty years old.

Those who are inclined to pause here in this delightful village to savour its peace and tranquillity could well add to their enjoyment by visiting the Italian-style church which contains work by Grinling Gibbons and some copper-gilt altar plate.

Fakenham 🍃

This is Robert Bloomfield country. His mother was born here in a cottage opposite the church and probably told him the ghost story that he made the subject of a poem. Apparently a local woman was crossing Euston Park on her way home when she heard footsteps behind her. Frightened, she began to run but the footsteps followed just as quickly. When she reached the cottage door, almost fainting with terror, she looked round to see what hideous spectre was behind and found it was a young donkey that had lost its mother.

'No goblin he, no imp of sin,
No crimes has ever known;
They took the shaggy stranger in
And reared him as their own.

His little hoofs would rattle round
Upon the cottage floor;
The matron learned to love the sound
That frightened her before.'

By chance another ghost story came to light in Fakenham in very recent years. Seven men employed by a London company to convert a row of four cottages into one residence met unexpected opposition to the work. According to the men, there were constant footsteps even when the floors were taken away. There were noises they could not explain and sometimes there were pieces of plaster flying about – altogether a place where they did not feel welcome. Their fright was so great that all seven men, in broad daylight, refused to enter the house again. There was much made of the affair by psychic sleuths determined to squeeze a ghost or two out of the story but like most tales of this kind it soon faded away. Perhaps if local country workers had been put in, the sort of men who know the tunes that old timber can play, it would have saved the ghost hunters a lot of time.

Farnham 🌿

The Farnham 'George' is the best-known landmark on this stretch of road between Wickham Market and Saxmundham. In front of its very door the road bends at almost a right angle and motorists are usually too busy negotiating the corner to take much note of the village. To be honest, there is very little there to notice – a number of houses around the George and a church at the top of a short hill, but it is well worth the visit at the expense of a few minutes from the course of a journey. The flint church with its tower of brick stands on an eminence that could not have been better chosen for the view it gives. The ground slopes gently down to the river Alde, narrow but visible from here as is the restless A12 road, somehow out of keeping with this quiet place. The church of St. Mary is simple and modest with high-backed pews.

The manor here originally belonged to Butley priory but came to the family of Glemhams when religious houses were reduced. Sir Thomas Glemham was M.P. for Aldeburgh and a staunch, fighting Royalist in the Civil War, together with two stalwart Suffolk neighbours, Colonel Gosnald of Otley and Major Naunton of Letheringham.

Sir Thomas secured the town of York for the king but had to acknowledge the gradually overpowering strength of the Ironsides. For his action on the king's side he was imprisoned at the end of the war. Later, he made his way to Holland to await the hoped-for Restoration but died before that came about.

Felsham 🌿

No wonder that Victorian servant girls spurned the neighbourhood of Mausoleum Farm when the shadows thickened in the evenings. For a hundred years or more there had been whispers about ghosts and unnatural happenings at the old castle there. It could hardly have been otherwise with queer John Reynolds defying the church as he did.

Reynolds was an eccentric, which did not prevent him from holding the high office of Sheriff of Suffolk and of having very set ideas on many matters. It was almost inevitable that he would find differences with the rector and he irascibly determined that he would have no further dealings with the church. Even the thought that the rector would benefit from funeral fees when he died irked him considerably and he decided to build his own mausoleum for himself and his family.

When the time came, John Reynolds was duly buried in his mausoleum in the grounds of the castle as were all the rest of the family. In the superstitious village life of the 18th century, the sequel was the reports of spectres and hobgoblins at the site, often elaborated into convincing tales. Certainly many bones were found there later on when the castle was demolished and a farmhouse built in its place.

Here at Felsham is the narrow stream taken to be the origin of the river Orwell. The village has a compact centre with shop and church side by side and situated in the good heavy land area south of Bury St. Edmunds. There was an airfield here in the last war and remains of the runways can still be seen.

There used to be a lamb fair until it was found that fewer and fewer lambs ever got to the market. Astute dealers would intercept drovers on the way and buy there and then in order to avoid the market dues.

Finningham

Prominent at every point in Finningham's past history is the name of Frere. In fact, a brass in the church records a whole list of them between 1736 and 1918 and as if this were not enough there are other monuments of other Freres from long before. The family came to settle here at the Hall in 1598. Since then many Freres have become Rectors of the parish, others have been administrators and civil servants of high rank. In Sir Henry Bartle Frere, the village provided yet another of those characters that seem to have flourished on Suffolk soil, the kind that could quite equably combine a life of tranquillity at home with occasional forays into far-flung parts of the empire.

Sir Henry's position in the Indian Civil Service somehow qualified him for a dangerous mission in Zanzibar at the height of the slave trade, and with due modesty he quickly produced a treaty in virtual settlement of the troubles and an end of slavery. So far, so good, but when Sir Henry was sent to South Africa during the Zulu risings he exceeded his brief and declared war on the tribes, for which he was suddenly recalled. The Empire received no further assistance from Sir Henry who never went abroad again but concerned himself with good causes at home.

Certainly the Frere family was good to the village in the terms that applied in those days which as in the giving of charity. No doubt the word charity was always distasteful but in desperate circumstances poor people had to swallow their pride, since charity was at least better than hunger. Eleanor Frere left a yearly sum of £12 to be taken from her estate and directed that it should be used in this way:- £4 for teaching six poor children to read and write, £5 for providing coats for four poor men who were regular church-goers, £2 5s. for meat to be distributed, 15s. for bread to be given out on the 12th of November. An earlier member of the family, Ann Frere, had left money for bread and for hempen shifts for the poor and for the teaching of four children.

The church here is of the 15th century, built on an earlier Saxon site of which there are now no remains. The tower is battlemented and there is some fine carving within. Windows commemorate Hatley Freres and Constantine Freres and, almost a stranger among so many of the same name here lies Sir John Fenn, High Sheriff of Suffolk and editor of the *Paston Letters*, remembered in a fine sculpture by John Bacon.

Flixton

Pride of place can be a very stubborn quality. Witness the sturdy villagers of Flixton near Lowestoft and the stout defenders of Flixton near Bungay. Only twenty miles apart and with exactly the same name, the two villages must often cause confusion, not so much for the inhabitants as for those who have to deal with deliveries and with administration. A few years ago a proposition was put before the two Flixtons – in view of the frequent mix-ups would one of them accept a change of name?

Never. Both said that the other could change its name but they wouldn't. Then would they accept a distinguishing suffix like Major and Minor or Upper and Lower? Never. Both Flixtons said that they were only prepared to be Major or Upper.

The suggestion was dropped. Both villages still have the same name and both are well pleased with the stand they made. No matter that at least one of them is so small that it is difficult to find it at all. In the case of Flixton (Lowestoft) one would conclude that they have really very little to fight for. There is but the ruin of a church which was demolished in a storm in 1703 and never rebuilt, a ruin whose consecrated materials were later used to repair some stables while the font itself served the purpose of a pig trough.

The lowest ebb for the village was at the count of 1602 when there were 2 inhabitants, a farmer and a shepherd. Long standing differences between the twin villages include disagreement over the origin of the name. Flixton comes from Felix, the first bishop of East Anglia, says the Bungay village. It is Danish and means Fliks Farm, maintain the others.

Fornham

Extraordinary things have happened at Fornham in the past and particularly in the tiny parish of St. Genevieve. Something of its story can be seen in the desolation of the tower still standing there and in the fine sword found under its walls in 1933 and which now reposes in Moyes Hall Museum in Bury St. Edmunds. Battles have been fought here and unfortunate accidents have happened as if fate had chosen these parishes for bizarre and unexpected events.

The most important of these – the great battle of Fornham – took place in the reign of Henry II. He was the king forever being betrayed by his ambitious sons and this battle was basically a family power struggle. When the Earl of Leicester joined the princes' cause it added considerably to their strength since he brought with him an army of Flemish mercenaries ready to do or die. The Earl landed at Walton and marched to Framlingham where the powerful Hugh Bigod welcomed him at the castle and helped to swell the rebel army. There were more recruits from Ipswich and at Haughley the troops captured a castle.

By this time, the king's trained soldiers were marching from the north under the leadership of Humphrey de Bohun, the King's

Constable and Richard de Lucy, Lord Chief Justice of England, to deal with the uprising. At Fornham, the rebels found themselves in imminent danger of attack and dug themselves in beside the Lark. The battle that followed was short and bloody with the disciplined, lance-bearing army of the king quickly subduing the Flemish hordes. The wife of the Earl of Leicester, a veritable Amazon who had insisted on being in the forefront of the battle, was taken prisoner. The Earl, however, initially escaped and gathered the remnants of his shocked and scattered army to make a last desperate stand close by the church of St. Genevieve. Here he was finally routed and thousands of Flemings died.

There is no sign of a battlefield now but the unearthing of that ancient sword with its haft inlaid with silver and carrying a Latin inscription is significant enough. Of a still earlier battle there is little evidence but mention is sometimes made of a desperate engagement between Edward, son of King Alfred and his uncle's son, whom he defeated.

Having suffered a battle under its very walls, the little church of St. Genevieve was subjected to more violence later on from an unexpected source. A man who was apparently shooting at jack-daws on the church steeple ignited the thatch by a wad that flew from his gun and on that day, 24th June 1782, the church was burned down. Only the tower remained as a lonely memorial.

Another unusual accident happened over a hundred years later when two men driving a heavy traction engine took a wrong turning somewhere and found themselves before the old bridge across the Lark. After an examination of the structure and consultations with passers-by the men decided that the bridge would be strong enough to support the engine. Unfortunately, it collapsed.

There was a priory here once, later pulled down and a house called The Priory built on the site. Nearby in Mermaiden Field were some ponds called the Mermaid Pits where some love-sick maid was said to have drowned herself.

Framlingham ❧

There is a comfortable, well-to-do air about Framlingham that derives to a large extent from the large and fertile farms in the area rather than to the limited tourist trade. It has a warm, rural charm and is included in this book as a village even though many may prefer to label it a town. The name itself has a pleasant sound and is supposed to come from the old river Fromus, which was described as beginning at Tannington and flowing to Marlesford where it joined the Gleme.

At the peak of the hill on which Framlingham stands is the great castle, a magnificent shell that hides the vacancy of its interior. Its origins are so old that it is simply assigned to the Saxon period. Perhaps the earliest drama that took place here was when Edmund, the young king of the East Angles, was besieged in the castle by the Danes until he escaped and made his way to Hoxne where he was recognised and murdered. The castle remained in the possession of the Danes for some time but in Norman days it was the subject of a gift from William Rufus to his friend Roger Bigod, the first of the powerful barons to reside there.

The most momentous year in the history of the castle was 1552. The young Edward VI had died and the country was split into two by the rivalling claims to the throne made by Mary Tudor and Lady Jane Grey. On July 10th Mary arrived at the castle, having proclaimed herself Queen rather prematurely since there was no certainty that she would be accepted. So finely balanced was the situation that Mary saw Framlingham both as a base and as a possible escape route to the continent should affairs go against her. With great determination, she ordered county sheriffs and loyal peers to rally to her side. Rally they did, to the total extent of 40,000 men. Sir Henry Bedingfield brought 140 of his own men, fully armed and trained and was appointed Knight Marshal.

Mary, 'that demonical and blood-stained princess' as one authority describes her, stayed at the castle until the end of July before marching to London. There, she received a tumultuous welcome.

A hundred years later the castle was subjected to extensive demolition for the purpose of road-making. For a description of the castle before this Cromwellian vandalism we have the expert eye of Dr. Henry Sampson, who was the rector of Framlingham at that time and also a local historian. He states:

'The Castle was very faire and beautifull, fortified with a double ditch, high banks and rampiers; the walls which are of great height and thicknesse, are strengthened by thirteene towers square built. The Castle was furnished with buildings very commodious and necessary, able to receive and entertaine many. In the first court was a very deepe well of excellent workmanship, compassed with carved pillars, which supported a leaden roofe. In the same court was a neat chappell, now wholly demolished and transported to the highways. On the west side of the Castle was a great lake reported to have once been navigable.'

Like an aged monarch anxious to keep up appearances, the castle presents an impressive exterior to the world. As we walk over the solid span that was once a drawbridge and under the portcullis, it is up to us to rebuild the chapel and the other parts of the ancient edifice with the bricks of our imagination. At least they cannot mend the roads with those.

Fressingfield ✎

The churchyard is as big as a park and no doubt well endowed with bones though there is only an occasional gravestone sticking up out of the grass and the eye is the more ready to look at the two buildings here. The church deserves most notice, its exterior massive but beautiful, 83 feet long and closely set with windows. The magnificent high porch was added to the church by Catherine de la Pole in the 15th century in memory of her husband and son, one killed at Harfleur and the other at Agincourt. Inside, there is a hammer-beam roof believed to be one of the best in Suffolk and there is much else that has survived since the church was built in the 14th century.

The pulpit was given as a memorial to a famous man, Archbishop Sancroft, who was one of the rebels of English history. He was born here at Uffords Hall, in the late 16th century, was educated at Bury St. Edmunds and went on to Cambridge and a theological career.

William Sancroft's elevation to the highest post in the Church came at a time of intense religious controversy. Troubles were brought to a head when the king sought to introduce an order intended to reduce persecution but the bishops resisted the right of the king to do so. The trial of the Seven Bishops acquitted the churchmen but Sancroft was in more trouble when he refused to take the Oath of Allegiance at the accession of William and Mary. He was deprived of office and suffered a sojourn in the tower of London. In 1690, he came back to Fressingfield and Uffords Hall as a broken old man of 72.

The other building on this eminence is a large, heavily-timbered house of the early 17th century. It was formerly the Guildhall and is now the Fox and Goose Inn. At one time there was also a school on the top floor.

Whittingham Hall also is not far away, the subject of many a story and local legend. One that is obviously true tells of Samuel Vince, a labourer at the Hall whose predilection for book-learning earned him an education which led him to become a foremost authority on mathematics and astronomy.

Another story is of the kind of which fairy tales are made but it has been recounted over and over again through the centuries. One day, we are told, the young prince who was to become Edward I was hunting near Framlingham when, after a heated chase he found himself near Whittingham Hall and called there for shelter and sustenance. There he saw Margaret, the beautiful daughter of the house and was so enamoured that he stayed at the Hall until angrily recalled by his father. The prince sought to protect his interests with the maid by asking the Earl of Lincoln to stay and guard her, for there were others seeking to ingratiate themselves. Two knights, one of Cratfield and the other of Laxfield, were already in love with Margaret and decided to settle their rivalry by a duel. By unhappy chance they were both mortally wounded.

The way was now open for the prince to pursue his courtship but he was urgently required elsewhere and could not return to Whittingham Hall for some time, during which Margaret, perhaps bemused by the excessive drama of so many suitors, decided to end the matter by marrying the Earl of Lincoln.

Freston

Freston greets you at the top of the hill that winds away from the Orwell no more than a couple of miles from the borough boundaries of Ipswich. At least, that is where the cheerful-looking Boot Inn stands but beyond that the houses are well scattered over the village. An ancient Hall once stood upon the hill, its lord of the manor one Fretson, who had taken his name from the village. In Tudor times it became the possession of the Latymer family.

It was sometime during the Latymer occupation, it is believed, that the tower was built which has aroused so much interest and curiosity since. It stands up among the trees and overlooking the river, a square, brick building six storeys high. The six rooms one above another measure 12 feet by 10 feet and are all connected by a winding staircase.

Mystery surrounds the tower for no one knows for certain who built it or why. The best thing about mysteries is that anyone is entitled to his own theories and there have certainly been a few fanciful ideas about Freston Tower. At least it seems obvious that the tower was intended to give views of the river and beyond for only the top storey is fitted with large observation windows and there is evidence that tapestry or other hangings were once used. The fact that the tower is divided into sections like rooms may be only incidental, perhaps to make the structure stronger.

As to who built this Tudor tower, it seems to have been conspicuously absent from a survey of the village in the reign of Henry VII so it seems safe to plump for the Latymers who lived at the Hall at the time of Henry VIII. There is an old belief that the arrangement of rooms was for a Latymer daughter to use a different one for each subject of her education. Perhaps astronomy in the top room?

Gipping ✒

Perhaps there is a special name for this strange malaise of the modern traveller which can only be described as a fear of side turnings. On any summer's day one can see sufferers from this disease taking their refreshment in dingy lay-bys close beside the noise and smell of traffic on busy roads, putting up with the devil they know rather than brave the lane that turns off into the unknown. It is a puzzling complaint. There is scarcely a side road anywhere that does not lead within a mile to some pleasant spot where the spirit as well as the stomach can find satisfaction. One could say that all that is best in the English countryside is up a side turning if we cared to take it.

Gipping has the authentic atmosphere of untroubled peace, a place where, as the saying goes, you can hear yourself think. The name comes from the name of the river because one of the three springs that serve the source is located here.

Well worth finding is the ornamental, small church with its walls and buttresses a fascinating pattern of flint work and stone. Inside, the nave and chancel are cheerful with light and colour from the huge windows. On the vestry doorway is an inscription in supplication of those who enter to pray for the souls of Sir James Tyrrell and his wife Anne of that line of Tyrrells so prominent in affairs good and bad through the ages. Perhaps few prayers have actually been said for Sir James in spite of his plea, for this is no other than the black-hearted murderer of the princes in the Tower. It is believed that the vestry was built by Tyrrell in remorse for the deed. Quite likely it was the very innocence of this quiet village that plagued his conscience most.

Glemsford 🖋

One of the largest villages in what used to be designated West Suffolk, Glemsford spreads itself handsomely between the Stour to the south and the wandering Glem to the east. Its size and prosperity has been due chiefly to the successful silk and wool weaving industry.

The ancient records of the village go back a thousand years to the reign of Edward the Confessor, when the See of Ely held most of the land here and set up a college of priests. With all the immense privileges granted to it, the college flourished throughout the Middle Ages. In the Domesday Book it shows that Odo, Earl of Champagne, held the manor at that time.

Inside the church of St. Mary is an oak reredos in memory of George Coldham, who was vicar here for 54 years but one can look in vain for mention of George Cavendish, who was buried here. Cavendish was the perfect gentleman's gentleman to no less a personage than Thomas Wolsey. No mere servant he, for he was usher, valet, confidante, friend and ultimately biographer. He accompanied the Cardinal in all the pomp and power of great events and as a faithful ally he shared the ignominy of disgrace. He had given up all to join the Cardinal when, at the age of 26, he left wife, children and home to assume the role he believed he was destined to fill.

When the Cardinal was seized in 1529 and shortly died, Cavendish was brought before a council of inquisitors perhaps frustrated that they had not had the opportunity to grill his master. He was examined and cross-examined with great hostility as to the life, habits and conversations of the Cardinal but in his honesty showed himself to be only a loyal servant and friend without knowledge or interest in state affairs. Cavendish was acquitted and retired to Glemsford to write his impressive biography.

Great Bealings

Side by side here are revealed the interests of the conservationist and the farmer. In the village generally, there is a great respect for trees although there are no extensive woods. Trees flourish in gardens and by the roadside and wherever there is space for one to grow. The result is a charming and leafy environment in which the axe is an abhorred implement. Perhaps the residents remember the story of the noble lord and his lady who lived at the Hall long ago. For some reason the husband decided that all the trees around the Hall must be felled but the lady, who was apparently a famous singer, used the charm of her voice and her tears to melt his resolution. It is two centuries since the Hall stood beside the church but the concern for trees goes on. Yet not far away are the familiar, bald roadside banks that border open spaces of land which cannot properly be called fields any more.

The great house here, perhaps one of the finest Elizabethan mansions in the county, is Seckford Hall, once the home of the wealthy court official, Thomas Seckford. His name is the first that newcomers to the district learn for Thomas believed that charity, like justice, should be seen to be done. The nearby town of Woodbridge has visibly benefited from his generous bequests. High up along one side of Seckford Street are the substantial almshouses that still look impressive and must have sheltered many hundreds of aged citizens in the long years since they were built. Further along Seckford Street used to be the Dispensary, where poor people could obtain free medical attention and medicines while close beside it was the Seckford Library where those who sought health for the mind could freely read and borrow from the wonderful collection of books.

Seckford Hall is well-used nowadays as a hotel but there was a long period when it was left to desolation and decay. How long it was I do not know but it was certainly deserted in my own childhood. In those days we used to walk down to the rough fields behind the Hall to pick blackberries and I can well remember how chillingly bleak and frightening it looked. We were convinced there were ghosts behind those dark windows and even in daylight we were glad to leave the Hall behind us. Now it looks as grand as it could ever have been, completely restored and a whole wing brought back to life after untold years of deterioration.

The arms of Thomas Seckford can be seen on the porch of the village church of St. Mary but there is little else in the way of memorial to this generous and far-thinking Elizabethan. A name that does seem prominent in local affairs is that of Moor, a family that lived at the very handsome Georgian mansion called Great Bealings House. The Rev. E. J. Moor was rector here from 1844 to 1886 but the best-known of that name was Major Moor, a great character of the last century. He had joined the East India Company when only twelve years old and had spent many adventurous years abroad in commerce and in the Army before retiring to enliven the affairs of Great Bealings.

Connected with the Major's occupation of Great Bealings House is the well-known story of the ghostly bells – a period of several days when the kitchen bells rang wildly at irregular intervals although there was no one in the rooms to ring them. The Major's friend, Bernard Barton, the Woodbridge poet afterwards wrote a satirical poem about the whole strange experience in which he offered several logical explanations. Barton was a frequent visitor to the house, as was Edward Fitzgerald.

Great Blakenham

Where Claydon ends and Great Blakenham begins is probably of little concern to the visitor except that it is about the common border line where the collection of local industries is based. In character perhaps, the works belong to Claydon rather than to Blakenham for the latter is obviously truly rural. It stands sleepily beside the old road from Ipswich to Bury St. Edmunds and beyond, which is now little used except for local traffic. No doubt it was the coming of the railway in 1846 that sparked off the idea of siting the industry here. King above all and first to arrive was the cement works whose tall chimneys can be seen for miles. Steel piling and

GT. BLAKENHAM CHURCH.

other enterprises followed but the conglomeration of works scarcely impinges upon the quiet nature of the area.

The church is plain but contains many items of interest, including a beautifully-decorated Jacobean pulpit and an ancient octagonal font. Norman remains from an earlier structure can be discerned in the structure. Another Norman installation in the village was a Benedictine cell of the alien monastery of Bec, which was removed by Henry VI. The manor of Great Blakenham was conferred upon Eton College which has retained the right up to modern times.

Groton

As stiff-necked himself as the church that drove him and his like away, John Winthrop lived to introduce as narrow a conception of religion in America as he had renounced in England. He was born here at Groton in the year that the Armada sailed into the Channel, the son of the first lord of the manor after the Dissolution of the Monasteries had dispossessed the Abbey of Bury St. Edmunds. Adam Winthrop died in 1562 and was buried here while his son John grew up to be a chest-beating religious zealot with the strict views of a John Bunyan. For all that, he rejected the opportunity to enter the church and became a lawyer, worldly enough to be a very successful one and to marry four times. There were fifteen children, doubtless all well-indoctrinated with fire-and-brimstone theology.

Religious persecution had already driven the Pilgrim Fathers to seek a new land and Winthrop was only one of 20,000 who about that time braved the Atlantic in their small, storm-tossed ships. However, some quality in John Winthrop earned him the post of first Governor of Massachusetts and he held on to this until his death in 1649. His government was stern and unequivocally concerned with his own concept of godliness and righteous behaviour. Soon after his appointment, a religious covenant was drawn up ensuring that only church members would be entitled to civil rights.

Winthrop, an outright Puritan if ever there was one, abolished all signs of frivolity as well as clothing fripperies such as lace. He regarded the days of the week and the names of months as idolatrous and made sure his followers were as much afflicted with sackcloth and ashes as he was. Just the same, he worked hard with his hands and was one of the most successful of the new colonists in setting Massachusetts upon the path of prosperity.

Grundisburgh

The charm of this village lies in its well-arranged compactness. It opens up to the stranger with an immediate identity that usually persuades him that he must stop and look around. A good decision, this, for here is the centrepiece of the green and all around it, spread idly from different periods of the past, are church and shop, school and public house, besides a sprinkling of houses. The school dominates, having a superior position overlooking the green where wooden footbridges cross the infant river Finn and the visitor is lured to the shady cedars beside the church. There is a seat and a war memorial showing that seven Grundisburgh men earned military honours during the war and a bus shelter facing the older-style houses of the village. Most of the new bungalows are tucked away along the narrow side-roads.

There is still an old forge here where horses from the heavy land farms round about used to come to be 'shod'. At one time a hundred horses depended on the smith for this service. Of the other local craftsmen, the basket-maker survived longest. The Pipe family have used their special skills for generations and I can remember very clearly how every week they used to drive a horse and cart loaded with clean, strong baskets of all kinds to the market at Woodbridge.

The church hides itself a little among the trees, perhaps embarrassed that its original tower fell and had to be built again in 1731. It is light and spacious inside and the eyes are lifted at once to the magnificent double hammer-beam roof of the nave, where whole rows of angels look down.

Along one of the narrow roads of the village is the large Baptist chapel that was extended in the last century to seat a thousand people. With two ministers, the chapel served those of a non-conformist persuasion from a total of thirty-six parishes.

There is considerable pride and sense of proprietorship in the village, even among those who are relatively new-comers, which includes all who have arrived within the last twenty years. With the older people there is much that is reminiscent of the days of more basic life-styles and of respectable servitude. No wonder, since as late as the twenties a small army of villagers worked at the Hall, at the large house called the Basts and nearby farmhouses. At the Hall there were 12 servants inside and 5 gardeners among the total then regarded as necessary and local life was affected very largely by the kind of man who was lord of the manor. Here the villagers were fortunate for the Gurdons, that became the Lord Cranworths, were sterling country gentlemen of the first degree. In neighbouring Culpho church is a tablet that says of the first Lord Cranworth: 'He was a gracious landlord and kind to all his tenants'. So far as village life is concerned, that is as good a memorial as can be given to anyone.

Hasketon ☙

Some people clap their hands to their ears at the very mention of church bells, while others find them uniquely satisfying to listen to. I must confess that I seldom notice them nowadays, probably because of traffic noise, but if I were to try to describe the atmosphere of the twenties and my own personal impressions at that time, the sound of Hasketon church bells would have to take a prominent part. Others who remember them have called it a 'sweet' sound. Certainly I can recall nothing so melodious and inspiring as the sound that came clearly from a mile away across the fields on a peaceful Sunday morning. To me, Hasketon bells gave the very sound of the twenties – quiet but jubilant.

The church still stands closely sheltered by beech trees but through the foliage you can see the round tower surmounted by its octagonal top. Across the road is the war memorial and not far beyond is a row of houses called Tymmes Place. Thomas Tymme deserved the memorial for he was a generous benefactor and in his will of 1614 made a variety of bequests from which generations of villagers have benefited. Others of the 'gentry' followed his example, in particular three women, Agnes Emme, Alice Osborne and Mary Brown. John Rutland left £3 a year to provide coats for three poor men.

Hasketon has not had the leavening of new country dwellers that some villages have had and one can still feel the divide that used to separate very clearly the people with land and those without. Even Thomas Tymme, for all his exemplary concern for the poor, would not have wanted any change in that arrangement.

Hawstead ☙

There was some doubt afterwards as to whether Queen Elizabeth was much amused by the follies set out for her at Hawstead Place on her visit in 1575. One of them, apparently, was a gross figure of Hercules in the water garden 'which discharged by the natural passage a continual stream of water into a stone basin.' A distinguished rector of Hawstead, Sir John Cullum, later gave it as his opinion that 'modern times would scarcely devise such a piece of sculpture as an amusing spectacle for a virgin princess.'

Affronted or not, the queen was known to be delighted when her silver-handled fan was recovered from the moat. The owner of the Place was knighted forthwith but doubtless for more substantial services than this.

The manor of Hawstead came to the Drurys in 1504 and the family left its mark on many aspects of social history before the line came to an end. Sir Robert Drury was elected Speaker in 1495 and in 1501 he obtained permission from the Pope to build a private chapel because the mile-long road to the parish church was 'subject to inundations and other perils.' One of his sons, Sir William, built the massive Drury House in London which gave the name to the adjacent Drury Lane. His brother, Dru Drury, was an Elizabethan courtier sent to Fotheringay Castle to keep Mary, Queen of Scots, in custody. Another Drury was killed in a duel.

An alabaster monument in the church commemorates the tragic death of Elizabeth Drury at only 16, a beautiful girl loved by a prince and also loved, to judge from his grief, by the poet, John Donne. He saw in Elizabeth's death all the frailty and impotence of mankind.

> 'Her pure and eloquent blood
> Spoke in her cheeks and so distinctly wrought
> That one might almost say her body thought.'

Helmingham

The vast estate of Helmingham, reckoned to be something like 6000 acres, came to the ancient family of the Tollemaches by way of marriage. In 1490 Lionel Tollemache married the rich heiress to the Helmingham's fortunes and established the unbroken association of family and village to the present day, although the former seat at Bentley was retained.

With wealth came titles. Queen Elizabeth I was pleased to confer a knighthood upon Lionel Tollemache and in the next generation another Lionel (most of the early eldest sons seem to have been named Lionel) received the title of baronet among the first to be so honoured. It was not until 1871 that a baronetcy was conferred

HELMINGHAM HALL
AND PARK
SUFFOLK

upon John Tollemache, who had succeeded to the estate some forty
years earlier. It was the first Lord Tollemache more than any other
who was responsible for the revolutionary lay-out of the village.
The first impression is of a demesne rather than a village as we know
them but it is a distinctly Victorian demesne with an atmosphere
that lingers from that period. Here, along all the roads that border
the great park are the well-spaced pairs of cottages built by the
baron before he received his title. They are firmly built and blend
perfectly with their environment, each one with half an acre of land
for corn and a pigsty. No doubt they were seen as model homes at
that time and fortunate indeed were those workers employed as
gardeners, foresters and farm men who could thus satisfy their
longing for a bit of land and the independence it allowed. There are
140 of these cottages, well spread out, with just an occasional
farmhouse for variation and the old forge still standing at the
road-fork.

The great house dominates all. From the splendid gateway to the
noble facade of the Tudor mansion the wide drive goes perfectly
straight, to rise a little before the house and point out the imposing
lines of the quadrangular building. The tall decorative chimneys of
the period reach upward to a benevolent heaven. All around it is the

spacious park of 375 acres, nicely sprinkled with casual trees of spreading habit and there is usually a glimpse to be had of deer and exotic wildfowl. Nowadays, when the park is open to the public, visitors can take 'safari' rides seated on a trailer behind a tractor to catch up with one or more of the deer herds.

The Tollemaches have been heroes as well as successful brewers. The beautiful small church standing at a corner of the park is naturally much given to memorials of the family. Here is one to the gallant young Lionel Robert Tollemache, born in 1774 and at 18 years old an ensign in the foot guards. At the outbreak of war with France he was killed at Valenciennes, still only 18 and the only officer to be lost in the battle.

The inscription goes on to tell of the bad fortune of some other members of the family: 'The name of Tollemache has been unfortunate! The father of, and two uncles of this gallant youth, like himself, lost their lives prematurely in the service of their country. His uncle, the Honourable George Tollemache, was killed by falling from the masthead of the *Modeste* man-of-war at sea. His father, the Honourable John Tollemache, was killed in a duel at New York. And another of his uncles, the Honourable William Tollemache was lost in the *Repulse* frigate in a hurricane in the Atlantic Ocean. So many instances of disaster are rarely to be met with in the same family.

> 'Thus fell the young, the worthy and the brave,
> With emulation view his honoured grave.'

This is a tidy, well-planned village in the light of Victorian standards and it maintains a quiet charm that goes well with the unassuming cottages and ample gardens. The uniformity does not pall but seems to provide a sense of placidity that is only occasionally broken by a passing horseless carriage.

Hemingstone

Elizabethan Hemingstone Hall enjoys a very pleasant corner here where Shrubland Park and pretty Coddenham are neighbours. The road becomes narrow after passing the Hall and it is easy to miss the even narrower side turning that becomes a short, steep hill to the church. St. Gregory looks a little lonely up here on its own and

84

perhaps a bit conscious of its age. There are still some signs of Saxon stone-work and the church was included in the Domesday survey but it is basically a 14th century edifice.

On the north wall is what looks like a secondary porch but was in fact an annexe especially built as a squint. At a time in the see-saw of religions when Protestantism was dominant, a local man named Ralph Cantrell determined to cling to his Catholic beliefs. The danger was that if he did not at least pay lip service to the English church he could find himself deprived of his lands and fortune. Cantrell accordingly built this small porch which became known as Ralph's Hole. Here he could see and hear the service without actually taking part and this seemed to satisfy his own conscience and the law.

The ribald type of humour of earlier centuries can be seen in the odd circumstances concerning another local landowner named Baldwin le Petteur. His title to the lands apparently depended on his appearance before the king on Christmas Day, when he was required to jump, to belch and to break wind. A similar rite was demanded of a native of Wattisham.

There were just four basic trades being carried on half way through the last century — shoemaker, tailor, blacksmith and wheelwright. Two of the local farmers were women and a few miles away at Henley the blacksmith was Mary Girling.

Hengrave

The lord of the manor had a Lancashire accent and a background of trade but it made no difference because his pockets were full of good English gold. He was Thomas Kytson, soon to be a knight, a merchant who dealt in expensive materials like satin, lace and velvet in a constant trade with Flanders. He made his fortune shrewdly but spent it lavishly, settling at Hengrave in the 16th century having created the stunning magnificence of the Hall, which was 13 years in the making.

Sir Thomas lies now in the more modest proportions of the parish church nearby but even now impresses the stranger with the great alabaster monument which seems almost to fill the chancel. There are other tombs too, to the Darcys and the Gages. At the time that the manor belonged to Lord Darcy, it happened that his beautiful second daughter was pursued by three equally eligible young suitors. They were Sir George Trenchard, Sir John Gage, and Sir William Hervey. Between them they made the girl's life an agony of indecision and on being importuned for the hundredth time she declared that she would marry them all. This in fact she did in that order as one after another died.

By her second marriage the manor came into the possession of the Gages. Sir John occupied himself mainly in writing a full history of Hengrave but he is also generally given the credit for introducing that succulent fruit, the greengage.

After several changes of owners, the Hall was put up for sale in 1952 and became a convent school for about twenty years, when it was handed over to the Church as an ecumenical centre.

Heveningham

The reason that most people have for going to Heveningham is to see the Hall. On prescribed open days a fair number of us will climb into our cars, solve with varying success the enigma of exactly where Heveningham is and indulge our curiosity about the great house and its grounds.

On a hot day the park itself is oasis enough and so spacious that a complete village could be enclosed there within its 600 acres should such an unlikely requirement ever occur. The hall overlooks the park with great dignity, revealing Corinthian columns and an extended facade. It was begun in 1778 by Sir Gerrard Vanneck of the noble family of Huntingfield and finished in what is regarded as a better style by Mr. James Wyatt.

More extraordinary was the ancient hall which the present one replaces. It was situated in a different part of the park and consisted chiefly of an immense central hall built around six great oaks. These living trees helped to support the roof as the branches grew upward and were also very convenient for the hanging-up of cross-bows, hunting horns and other bric-a-brac of the time.

Throughout their occupation of the Hall, the Huntingfields have continued their interest in tree planting and maintenance and the entire area is impressively wooded with new and aged hardwoods of every kind. A famous tree here was the Queen's Oak, from whose shelter Queen Elizabeth I is credited with having shot a buck. The oak was almost eleven yards in circumference.

The park is divided into roughly equal halves by the rivulet of the Blythe, which has also been used to create a fine lake before the house. Nearby, the modest church displays the arms and the memorials of the Huntingfield family as well as the grand pew screened for their private devotions.

Hintlesham ❧

Half way along the winding road between Ipswich and Hadleigh is the pleasant small village of Hintlesham, with its flint-towered church standing close beside the highway. Just beyond the next bend is the tree-flanked gateway to the Elizabethan mansion of Hintlesham Hall. It was built by the Timperleys who occupied it until 1740 and there are many memorials in the church to point to the virtues and valour of this family. One monument on the north wall is to Captayne John Timperley who was killed in 1629 and it displays all the equipment and arms of a soldier of that time. It was erected by his wife, who declared: 'this memoriall is too too little to expresse either his deserte or her affection'. There are also monuments to the Deane family which supplied a succession of long-serving rectors and to the Misses Lloyds. Miss Harriet was the last of the magnanimous Lloyd sisters who died in 1837.

The beautiful, chaste-looking facade of the Hall with its high Tudor chimneys has become a familiar rendezvous for many people in recent years since it was taken over by Robert Carrier. This well-known chef and gourmet converted the Hall to a Hotel and a training ground for would-be cooks. Earlier in this century the village knew well the figure of Havelock Ellis as he walked the lanes nearby. Though he had started life as a ship's boy, since his father was a sea-captain, he rejected the prospect of becoming a mariner after a particularly long and galling voyage to Australia in the 1870s. Back on land, he dedicated his energies to writing on the subjects of sex and psychology, creating a good deal of controversy as he did so. He died here in 1939.

Hitcham ✑

This is a large and straggling village about equidistant from Hadleigh and Stowmarket. It is John Stevens Henslow's village as surely as Selborne is Gilbert White's. Henslow was rector here for about twenty years and brought enlightenment, scientific curiosity as well as fame to this backward community which at first had only contempt and resentment for the new parson. Had they known that he was Professor of Botany at Cambridge University and lectured to learned societies it would have made no difference. Stubborn ignorance on the part of the labouring families and suspicion from the farmers made the professor's first attempts at social reform very difficult but it did not deter him for an instant from his plans for the village.

Poverty was obviously the first difficulty, then lack of education, then lack of independence – Henslow tackled everything from the beginning, arranging thrift clubs, building a school for parents as well as children, planning ploughing matches and trying to secure land for allotments. There was outraged opposition to all. As soon as the school was established, the professor organised special classes in botany for the village children, an idea so successful it was later taken up by education authorities all over the country.

Soon, he began his famous botanical excursions, first with children to areas where collections could be made and plants examined. Later, parents and farmers and all would join the expeditions. The climax of these outings was the one when nearly 300 people went from the village to Cambridge and Henslow explained the work he was doing there. As if this was not enough to strike awe into the party, there to welcome them was the Vice Chancellor, who ushered them into Downing Hall to partake of plum pudding and beer.

Of all Henslow's honours, perhaps the most rewarding was the silver cup that the local farmers gave him for his advice and help with their problems.

Holbrook ✑

The tall, graceful tower of the Royal Hospital School dwarfs all else in the village. It is 200 feet high, beautifully graduated and visible for many miles around. About its feet are the main buildings of the establishment, dedicated to the Navy-style training of young boys. For 50 years the presence of the school has dominated the area, with something like 1,000 boys in residence together with the requisite staff. At the time that the original Royal Hospital School was founded in 1821, it was intended that just 10 boys who were sons of seamen should receive free education. In 1759 the first school was built and in 1933, by now a major educational institution for the Navy, was moved to Holbrook. Building had already been going on here for 5 years and the site stretched for half a mile. There were 11 separate school houses named after famous naval commanders of the past and each house accommodated 80 boys.

Apart from the spectacular central tower, a feature of great pride to the school is the chapel, full of colour and light. Marble is used both in the main area and in the lady chapel where a brilliant mosaic forms a memorial to the school's benefactor, Gifford Sherman Reade.

Mr. Reade was a patriot who had greatly admired the exploits of the Navy in the Great War. When he decided to try a new life in New Zealand, he relinquished the vast estate of 860 acres between the Stour and the Orwell which had been his family's and gave it to the Admiralty.

There was no official opening of the school but the foundation stone was laid by the Duke of York, afterwards George VI, in the entrance hall. It is believed that the buildings will last for a thousand years, with such strength was the structure made over an immense depth of reinforced concrete.

Hollesley

The church stands beside the tiny village centre in what seems to be a piece of wasteland. It has no porch but the arrangement of large flints and stone-work make the exterior walls look very handsome. It is worth the visit in order to see the great variety of carvings on the pew-ends, the most elaborate I have seen. They are chiefly of animals and birds, many of them of devilish aspect with tails and claws occupied in attacking and gouging their prey. There is a sciapus on its back with its huge webbed feet over its head and there are also peaceful cameos of harvest scenes.

Nearby are a few modern houses mingling with the old and sharing the keen air that blows here across the open marshes by the sea. Just outside the village is the long-established Hollesley Bay Colony, to use its original name. It is now a Borstal centre. The rather bleak landscape here is given over to crops and orchards that are maintained by the inmates. As early as 1900 there was what was called a Colonial College here. In the Illustrated London News of 1905 is a description of the College where the unemployed were sent to be trained for farmwork at home and abroad. At that time there was much encouragement for single men to emigrate to Canada or Australia.

Close by is the road that leads across the open marshes to Shingle Street and the sea. It is a corner of the coast that has never changed — just an expanse of shingle beach on which a handful of houses stand, with a Martello tower for company. The houses still seem to cower from the winter's gales even in the summer. Overhead the curlews call across the lonely marshes and beside the single road the bull-rushes are forever whispering.

Honington

Pastoral poets around here would have their musings sadly interrupted nowadays by the sound of aeroplanes belonging to the nearby base but in the 18th century Honington was a hamlet of tranquillity and charm. Some of that atmosphere, as of being half-forgotten in these rural backwaters, still lingers among the lanes here and it is possible to imagine what it was like for Robert Bloomfield, the peasant-poet who was born in 1766. His early, formative years were spent here and though he was later destined to leave the village it was always of Honington and its neighbourhood that he wrote, perhaps all the more poignantly because of his exile.

Robert went to work on a nearby farm at a tender age but as events turned out, soon found himself learning a trade far from home. His mother kept a small school in Honington but the large family was poor and it seemed expedient to send Robert to join his brother in London and become a shoemaker. There he shared a garret with several other apprentices but somehow managed to write his best-known work, *The Farmer's Boy*, after the emotional experience of returning to his native village for a spell in 1786.

With the success of his poems, the Duke of Grafton became his patron and found him a comfortable job in the sealing office. After a time, bored and unhappy, with none too robust health, he returned to work as a shoemaker, tried the book trade and became a bankrupt. He died in poverty in a village of Bedfordshire.

A serious fire once occurred in Honington that threatened to destroy his mother's cottage. Luckily it was saved and later renovated, some say with little respect for the original. There is a modest memorial in the church, fitting for this unassuming countryman who was also the very voice of our native fields.

Hoxne

Here was the martyrdom of the young hero-king, Edmund. He was crowned when only 15 years old and like Alfred of Wessex, he was pious yet brave, forever sought peace and found no triumph in victory over an enemy. In 870 AD the Danes were pressing forward across East Anglia despite King Edmund's efforts towards peace and at Thetford a battle became inevitable. At length the Danes prevailed, Edmund was driven back to Hoxne where he attempted to re-group his followers but, seeing that there would only be more blood spilt, he finally gave in and was taken prisoner. Perhaps, being magnanimous himself, he hoped that the Danes would prove likewise but they demanded terms in exchange for his life. He would have to yield up half of his kingdom, he would occupy the throne merely as a puppet of the Danes and he would have to renounce his faith.

When King Edmund refused, he was bound to an oak tree, whipped and attacked with arrows. The arrows struck him relentlessly:

> 'No place for wounds remained, the savage crew
> As thick as winter hail their arrows threw.'

At the end his head was struck off and thrown down among the bushes. Legend comes in here with the carrying off of the head by a wolf and later, when the body was disinterred, it returns with the story that the head had become miraculously rejoined. A rough chapel of sawn trees and thatch was built over the grave and he lay there where he had fallen for 33 years before being removed to the town which was to become Bury St. Edmunds. A cell of the Benedictines was established later on the site with seven monks and a prior dedicated to prayer for St. Edmund, king and martyr. After the Dissolution, a mansion was erected here.

Another story of Edmund's conflict with the Danes may also be legend rather than fact, though it is often repeated. It is about an incident when the king was sheltering under a bridge out of sight of his enemies. A young couple who were about to be married were crossing over the bridge and caught sight of the king's golden spurs reflected in the water. According to the tale, the king was betrayed to the Danes and forthwith cursed the bridge and all wedding couples who crossed it. For long centuries after, the fear of the curse kept would-be-weds well away from what came to be known as the Gold Bridge.

The old oak believed to be that of Edmund's martyrdom fell something like a thousand years later. Here again, fact or legend found an arrow head deeply embedded in the wood, and it has been seen as likely enough to be one of those shot at the king as to justify preserving the block of wood in which it was found.

Hoxne has a special charm in its situation here beside the Waveney where the little Dove joins in. The village is only a few miles from Eye and Diss but is off the main traffic roads and manages to retain a genuine rural atmosphere with its quiet lanes and interesting old houses. Flax growing and milling was once much encouraged here and a mill on the Waveney that had been doing service as a corn mill was at one time converted for dealing with the more profitable flax.

Icklingham

The joint parishes of St. James and All Saints form the community of Icklingham, which ranges for about a mile on the north side of the Lark. Here was an important Roman settlement and the two churches have been used from time to time to house the abundance of bricks and tiles and other remains which have been ploughed up in nearby fields. The bricks particularly are of much interest because of their great variety in shape and pattern, some with rough tracings of animals and flowers and some obviously having been vitrified. Apparently the settlement extended for about half a mile and not far from the river. There is a visible 25-acre square called Kentfield which some say is a corruption of Campfield. Coins, kitchen utensils and a lead cistern large enough to contain 16 gallons of water have been found here.

Near the point where the village boundary touches the neighbouring parishes of Elveden and Eriswell is the spectacular memorial to the dead of all three villages in the Great War. It was set up here among the trees in 1921 by Lord Iveagh.

The two churches are about half a mile apart, with towers of flint where gargoyles, particularly on St. James, leer down as you enter. All Saints is the older church, with some recognisable Norman remains in the 14th century edifice and it contains much of interest including an ancient metal-bound chest and what was once a three-decker pulpit.

Ickworth

Although Ickworth Hall is now one of the show-pieces of Suffolk, there was a time during the building of it when it was abandoned and it threatened to become a ruin. The many visitors to the Hall can feel satisfaction that the project was eventually completed for here is a striking piece of architecture of fairly recent times. It consists chiefly of a large, oval centre-piece and two long wings that altogether extend to something near 700 feet. The imposing centre is almost circular, being 120 feet north and south by 106 feet east and west. It is capped by a dome which carries the height to 100 feet. There are classical references in its style, with columns of Ionic and Corinthian design and there are friezes carrying in relief the stories of the Iliad and Odyssey.

The ancient family of Herveys live here, its head no longer generally known by that name but as the Marquis of Bristol. The estate came to the Herveys by way of marriage. John Hervey was created a peer in 1703 by Queen Anne at the insistence of the Duchess of Marlborough and in 1714 he became the Earl of Bristol. The fifth earl, Frederick William Hervey, F.R.S., was made a marquis in 1826.

In the 18th century the Earl of Bristol was a great art collector and an admirer of Italy. As a consequence, he was inclined to spend long sojourns in that country while at the same time he was beginning the project at Ickworth with the object of having a great house as a repository for his works of art. Unfortunately, the Earl's collection abroad was taken by the French in 1798 and he was confined for a time in an Italian prison. Such events upset the Earl's plans and he apparently abandoned Ickworth to its fate and spent the rest of his life in Italy. He died in 1803, having disposed of his remaining works of art apparently to strangers.

At that time only part of the centre-piece and the bare foundations of the wings had been done and for about 20 years nothing more happened. It was something of a problem for the new Earl who at first favoured clearing the site. Eventually he decided to go ahead and completed the Hall with the success obvious to all who see it.

Perhaps even more wonderful than the Hall is the park in which it stands. It is said that a whole parish was enclosed within the park which is 11 miles around the outer edge. Herds of deer roam here under the great trees and in a corner stands the fine old church in which the Herveys have been buried.

Kedington

From long usage the name of Kedington has been reduced to Ketton in local speech, much to the dismay of those who see Kedington as a very special place. Lavish admiration has been bestowed, not so much upon the village but upon the great church. Someone once called it the 'Westminster Abbey of Suffolk' and the phrase is often heard. 'The most beautiful church in any county in England' declared Sir Alfred Munnings, while a more cautious appraisal by a Suffolk architect concedes that 'it is one of the most interesting churches in the county.' Other people, to be fair to rival churches, have found the edifice 'gloomy' and 'uninspiring'.

The church register dates from 1654 and the chancel is 14th century with the nave probably a hundred years later. There is a magnificently ornate 'squire's pew' and a three-decker pulpit but the interior is dominated by the monuments and inscriptions to the Barnadiston family, who were lords of the manor, squires and landowners for as long as history can recall. Certainly they were here long before the church and indeed they had a hand in the building of it. It is believed that there were Barnadistons in

Kedington before the Norman conquest. The earliest effigies in the church are those of Sir Thomas who died in 1500 and his wife who died in 1520. Through the centuries other Barnadistons have been added to the family vault. Last of all was Sophia who died in 1855.

The Barnadistons were against the king in the Civil War but changed with some alacrity at the Restoration in 1660 when Samuel Barnadiston gave such assistance to the king as to earn himself an immediate knighthood. It was Samuel, in his youth, whom Queen Henrietta saw from her window in the early days of the conflict and remarked: 'See what a handsome round head he has.' This is said to be the origin of the term 'Roundheads' for the Parliamentary forces but it could equally well have come from Captain David Lyde's scathing comment that they were 'round-headed, crop-eared knaves.'

Whether he was the original Roundhead or not, certainly Samuel seemed frequently to be concerned in troubles with the authorities. Judge Jeffreys fined him £10,000 on one occasion for writing a malicious criticism of the Rye House Plot proceedings. For failing to pay this vast sum, Samuel was imprisoned for four years.

Kelsale

Less than fifty yards away the cars chase each other's tails along the A12 towards Lowestoft and Yarmouth. Yet here, an old man can sit on a bench in the sun and see a village that has kept its rural charm. Somehow, Kelsale drops an invisible curtain on the world of today and carries on as it always did. The old Guildhall dominates the tiny village centre, with its timber frame handsomely accommodating teachers nowadays on their meetings and courses. Once it was a school and before that a shelter for paupers. Opposite the Guildhall is the Eight Bells Hotel, just as ancient and well timbered.

Wander a little further and there are small bridges over almost non-existent streams that lead past close-grouped rows of charming houses to a short, steep hill. Here, in a commanding position on the grassy mound is the church, quiet and tree-sheltered and introduced by way of a lych-gate of magnificent size and construction. Faces and creatures look down from the battlements of the tower and below there are still two Norman arches over doorways. Dowsing paid a visit here and recorded: 'We brake down 6 superstitious

Pictures and took up 12 Popish inscriptions in brass; and gave orders to level the chancel and taking down a cross.'

The village has been well cared-for in the past, with great concern for the poor and for the education of its children long before schooling became compulsory. An amalgamation of charities provided money for apprentices and even for scholars to go to University. From these funds a schoolmaster was paid £50 a year to teach 90 boys. He was also required to teach Sunday School but was provided with a house and garden, should he ever have the leisure to work on it.

Kersey

Pride of place is a fine virtue when tempered with moderation. Too much of it can turn a village that is simply picturesque into self-conscious preciousness. Eulogies of praise and admiration have been showered upon the beauties of Kersey. It has the burden of being frequently elected the prettiest village of England. Indeed, when Lord Woodbridge opened the new village hall after the Second World War he felt that such a description was limiting and declared that it was the prettiest village in the world. It is a relief that such adulation cannot go any further unless cosmology succeeds in sending us pictures of villages on the planets.

Because of such high approbation, residents naturally feel a special kind of responsibility for the general appearance of the village. There was the awkward invention of electricity, for instance. For most villages it was something that was welcome and overdue. For Kersey it was the sound of doom. If people did not actually tremble in their beds at the prospect of poles and wires in the street, that is certainly the impression that the stranger must get, knowing that an emotional conflict went on for fifteen years.

When at last electricity came to Kersey in 1949, it arrived with a bally-hoo similar to that at the switching-on of Blackpool's illuminations. In Kersey only 20 houses were to benefit but there were crowds to cheer the official lighting-up and a great banner that said: 'This Switch Will Make History'. Simple people who only wanted electricity and not history had their electric bulbs and gadgets ready. All twenty houses were suddenly lit up.

In the same year, with the war far behind us, more history was made with regard to the village water supply. Until then there had been just two public pumps and one of these suspect, so that most people and the school had to go to the Rectory for water. Now this source threatened to dry up, the school was already waterless and it was at last decided to put a public stand-pipe near the church gate. Beauty has much to answer for.

The oldest cottages here once held looms for the weaving of Kersey cloth, which is mentioned two or three times in Shakespeare and nearby Lindsey produced what came to be known as Linsey Woolsey. Two hillsides form the village street with a stream crossing the road at the bottom. At the peak of one hill stands the church while upon the other are the ruins of a priory. The church looks very majestic there with the battlemented tower facing down the hill between the houses. It was built in the 14th and 15th centuries, the gap possibly being accounted for by the Black Death which interrupted the work on a good many Suffolk churches. There has been a continued restoration over the centuries which has not changed the original grace and power of the edifice. As recently as 1970 the bells were re-hung on a new frame and the fabric repaired. The beautiful south porch shows panelling and carving that is 500 years old.

Kesgrave

Kesgrave 'Bell' and the church have long been close companions, once in some isolation beside the road that led across the heath to Ipswich, nowadays with ample company as the area continues to expand. Only a wall separates the provision of physical sustenance from that of the spiritual and the two buildings share the shade of the same cedar trees. The proximity is explained by the fact that the 'Bell' was built on the site of a Rest House, a religious centre associated with Butley Abbey. Tudor influence is visible in both church and inn, the latter with its heavy beams and the former showing the Elizabethan red bricks of the tower. The church welcomes the visitor and the worshipper into an impressive north porch with trefoil-headed windows and into the nave whose well-timbered roof is now bereft of 18 cherubims that Dowsing saw fit to remove.

Outside, the cedars shade an unusual grave and memorial. It is the tomb of John Chilcote, a horse-dealer of Woodbridge, and the carving on the stone depicts a man holding a horse with another man with a whip standing behind. Chilcote was only 25 when he died in 1851, apparently from the Victorian scourge of consumption and his two sisters joined him there when they fell to the same disease. One of the sisters was Repronia Lee, wife of a gipsy king.

Not far away is the grave of John Dobbs, an unhappy shepherd who hanged himself in a barn and was buried with a stake through his body. A cross still marks the spot beside what was once a cross-roads. By tradition, the grave was tended by whoever was the local shepherd.

For all its size, Kesgrave still has much of the atmosphere of any village. Suffolk people live here and many use the lazy sounds of the dialect. At the same time, an urban vitality is obvious in the diverse activities that take place, much of it to the benefit of local institutions.

I spent two very enjoyable years living in Kesgrave and came to realise that the old phrases 'ribbon development' and 'bungaloid growth' had no justification here. What may have been roadside building at first has been developed in depth into a complete conurbation. In it, many thousands of people live quietly and contentedly in their separate bungalows and gardens, happily poised between town and country.

Kessingland

How are the mighty fallen! Once, Kessingland could have taken on neighbouring Lowestoft with one hand tied behind its back and won. Now, everything indicates that it is merely a satellite of the flourishing seaside resort. The great number of houses and bungalows built in Kessingland since the war does nothing to change this opinion for these are largely people who sleep here but work elsewhere. Not that Kessingland is not itself flourishing in a changed and minor role chiefly concerned with the holiday trade.

But this is trifling compared to its importance in the Middle Ages. With a population then of about 8000 mostly dependent on the port and herring fishing, it was busy enough to have a weekly market and an annual fair. At the time of the Norman Conquest, when Kessingland was required to pay a toll of 2200 herrings from its sea-harvest, Lowestoft was not even mentioned. Then, as at Blyth-burgh, the fortunes of the port declined as the harbour silted up. Nevertheless, it has always provided some of the finest herring fishermen along the coast, some of them manning the boats at Lowestoft.

Brave men and strange men have lived here beside the sea. There was Edward Wigg, lifeboatman and head of generations of lifeboatmen and Harry Smith, winner of the Stanhope Medal for the bravest deed of 1926 when he dived overboard in a storm and managed to save the life of a fellow crewman. There was Sea Row Jack, a man of means who chose to dress in skins and live in a wooden tower on the beach. In the close-knit community also lived Tidley, Bucko, Ike, Mouse, Yaller Iron, Spuff and Wonney among many other fishermen with nicknames.

Until the Dissolution of the Monasteries there was a great church here, looked after by the nuns of St. Clare. It fell into ruins and was replaced in the 17th century by a smaller church with a thatched roof.

Kirton

There has been a considerable invasion into Suffolk villages by newcomers since the Second World War and Kirton is one of those surprised to find itself suddenly twice as big as it thought it was. It has an ideal position here just four miles from Felixstowe with its busy port yet managing to keep the look and feel of an old-time community. Past the tiny green with its shop, pub and old black-smith's shop one can walk right down to the Creek, an inlet of the Deben where once ferries crossed the river to Ramsholt and Sutton. Kirton Sluice it is called and it gives no hint now of its history, for, apart from the square, man-made little harbour, there is nothing left visible but the remains of an old barge. Once it was a sizeable port with many ships coming up the river and there is still a local belief that ships to face the Spanish Armada were built here.

The church of St. Mary and St. Martin lies pleasantly at the end of a side road from the village centre. It was mentioned in the Domesday Book but has nothing antiquated about it nowadays. The influence of new blood and new ideas can be seen at a glance. A beautiful porch, more properly known as an entrance hall, welcomes the visitor into what could be the foyer of a first-class hotel but succeeds in blending perfectly with the main body of the church. Besides the new entrance, a great many improvements have been made and a church hall built nearby in which an astonishing number of village organisations are active.

A Bronte-type young woman lived here in the 18th century. She was Clara Reeve, a daughter of the rector and a determined writer who succeeded in getting her books published and indeed widely read by the standards of the time. A more recent character to inhabit the rectory was the Rev. J. W. Weir, known far and wide as a man who answered only to his own conscience and who was indefatigable in his work for the less fortunate in our society.

At the White Horse inn they will tell you of what was once the great joke of the village. One can imagine weather-beaten faces breaking into smiles as they heard it for the first time and enjoying it all over again when they were able to repeat it to someone else. The village, it was said, was held together by rivets. Yes, by Rivetts. There were more Rivetts here than any other name, at one time with twelve large families. Truly enough, the village was held together with Rivetts.

Knodishall 🪴

At one time it was Knodishall-cum-Buxlow, but the latter has long since disappeared. Knodishall itself was given in the Domesday Book as being simply a hamlet of Saxmundham.

An open, windswept appearance can be detected here as is the case with many heath-land communities. In the centre of the village a mixture of dwellings surround an area which can hardly be called a green since it consists chiefly of head-high furze and whin but which is somehow quite appropriate to this corner of Suffolk. About a mile from this spot is the off-shoot community of Coldfair Green, unusual in that the houses, though varied in style, form a long, close-set row beside the road.

Between the two communities the church of St. Lawrence presents an exterior that has little to delight the eye and is without a porch. Inside, however, it has its treasures, including a fine, carved Jacobean pulpit and a rare Early English font, whose octagonal bowl rests in splendid simplicity upon eight pillars. There are many memorials to the Jenneys family, a name believed to be a corruption from the French and certainly the Jenneys seem to have been lords of the manor here directly from Norman times to the middle of the 18th century. The original manor-house was long ago destroyed by fire.

Lavenham ✺

Lavenham is probably the best-known village in Suffolk. Like Snape, it is the right sort of place to know. Like Kersey, it suffers a little from too many panegyrics of praise. I sometimes wish that visitors to these proper places would spare a little time to go also to the more typical villages around.

Lavenham is unique, of course, as an exhibition of medieval architecture. Where else could you find such a magnificent church in company with beautifully timbered houses? But there are no warts on this face of the Middle Ages, only well-preserved perfection. It is an idealised picture that arouses some indignation if anything exists to spoil it. An ardent admirer of Lavenham (in an analogy of Beauty and the Beast) writes: 'The church, of course, is the Beauty and wondrously beautiful it is but the thing that is incredible is that nobody has planted a row of trees or a glorious high hedge to hide the ugly rows of houses looking at the church.' Do people really want a town to be a museum? Perhaps some do. Others may reflect that wool towns were not all timbered mansions but had their hovels too, or the merchants would not have become rich.

The famous church looks impressive in its size and its perfect situation. It was built with freestone and decorative arrangement of flints in the 15th and 16th centuries at the expense of the Earl of Oxford, lord of the manor here and the Spring family, with some help from Simon Brand. Thomas Spring was the renowned 'rich clothier' who made an immense fortune from the wool trade as did others in lesser degree. There were suitable private pews for these notables and around the church a number of memorials and inscriptions to the Springs.

Even more striking than the church, perhaps, is the wealth of memorable architecture round about. Here are the houses of the wool merchants, the Wool Hall and the incomparable Guildhall, with whole rows of medieval and Tudor houses of less importance.

The basis of the prosperity that provided these buildings was originally the weaving of blue cloth and serge. Later, the trade continued in serge, shalloons, says, stuffs, calimancoes, hempen cloth and worsted yarn. There was also straw plaiting. For the regulation of the trading standards there were three guilds or companies – St. Peter, Holy Trinity and Corpus Christie, governed by six burgesses chosen for life.

There were two annual fairs. One, that lasted for four days from October 10th, was for butter and cheese, the other for horses was held on Shrove Tuesday.

Laxfield

It comes as a surprise in this area of small villages between Framlingham and Stradbroke to arrive at Laxfield, for it is large enough to have a long and pleasantly wide village street. There is an invitation to pause here, if only to gaze on the variety of dwellings, side by side as many are, but completely independent in style. This is not all, however, for there are many things to see here and many things to enjoy. The whole place retains an unmistakable atmosphere of old Suffolk. In this long street one can imagine a blacksmith and a wheelwright still plying their trade and a tumbril or two rumbling on their tall wheels towards the farms. I know that Laxfield likes to think of itself as progressive and so it is, but it also holds on to its past in a very positive way. Not many communities of this size have a museum and certainly not such a one as this, beautifully housed in the Guildhall and staged openly beneath the ancient beams by dedicated local people. Yet Laxfield has this and more for many organisations make use of the building.

The ancient Guildhall dates from 1461 and was first called the Cherchehous. Its religious connections aroused the disapproval of Henry VIII and it was given into the keeping of the lord of the manor. At one time it was used as a parish workhouse.

The very impressive church is the work of different centuries but there was a church here in Saxon days and it was mentioned in the Domesday Book. The present fine 100 foot tower was erected in 1480 when a good deal of money accrued from local legacies. Inside the church is a splendid disposition of ancient and modern timber, some of it beautifully carved. Notices on the two groups of pews once separated men from women. The Jacobean pulpit has a reading desk at its base, completing what was known as a two-decker.

There is also a Strict Baptist Chapel here. Between the church and the chapel there has been a considerable interchange over the years, due apparently, rather to the convenience of marriage partners than to any serious change in belief. One man whose belief was constant unto death was John Noyes, a Laxfield shoemaker who refused to deny the reformed religion. He was imprisoned at Eye and at Norwich before being brought back to the village to die at the stake on 22nd September 1557.

Laxfield has a right to be proud of its past and of its present status but if there is anything of which it is slightly ashamed it must be that it gave house-room to the arch-vandal William Dowsing, born and bred here to become the lackey of the Commonwealth. He was appointed to rid the churches of 'superstitious' objects and pictures, which included the pictures in stained glass windows. No one could have carried out these orders more thoroughly. In 50 days he visited 150 churches and left a trail of havoc.

Perhaps there should have been a reckoning for this man at the time of the Restoration but he craftily made himself scarce, lying low in the village here for the remainder of his life.

Letheringham ✿

It is worth following the winding roads west of Wickham Market to find this pleasant but tiny village on the river Deben. Nearby are the ruins of a 14th century priory and the church, both relics of a past age for the chancel of the church has gone and the priory gateway that remains gives no more than a hint of its early importance as a cell of the Black Canons of Ipswich. It was Sir Robert Naunton, Secretary of State under James I, who took over the priory after the Dissolution and turned it into a mansion, complete with moat. The Naunton family lived here for several generations until after moving from Alderton but eventually the estate devolved upon William Leman, who dismantled much of the old Hall. It is now a farmhouse.

There is a water mill still standing beside the Deben here and it makes a favourite beauty spot in the summer. On dark nights when the wind howls it would probably have less appeal for it is known that a number of skeletons were found in the miller's garden in 1844. The story is that the murders were committed by an enraged ex-employee of the miller named Jonas Snell. At that time a Mr. Bullard and his son were running the mill and were both killed but Snell was soon caught and was executed at Wickham Market six weeks later.

Lidgate

When the ancient castle that stood on a mound here fell into disuse, its ruins were speedily used to repair medieval roads. In its place arose the handsome church of St. Mary, that could not have been more than a century old when it gave sanctuary and hope to a nameless boy. He was to be John Lydgate, who took the name of the village for his own and made it resound throughout the land.

John was fortunate among his contemporaries. He was given his early education at the monastery of Bury St. Edmunds and because of the promise that he showed was sent to Oxford, after which he went travelling abroad. He was much influenced by the authors that he admired so much; Boccaccio, Dante and especially Chaucer who was about 30 years older than he. With literary leanings himself, Lydgate sometimes sent his poems to Chaucer for his approval. His stature never reached that of the author of the *Canterbury Tales* but nevertheless he fills a distinct place in the progress of English literature.

Lydgate's literary energy was vast. For his patrons, who included both Henry V and Henry VI, he would turn out ballads, hymns and poems as required for masque or may-game or mumming. Apart from this he was usually engaged in writing vast screeds of poetry. One poem, called the *Falls of Princes* was nine times longer than Shakespeare's Hamlet. Perhaps they were read by a few people at a time when Chaucer had whetted their appetite for literature. But the promise of the 'monk of Bury' as he called himself was never fulfilled save in his tireless industry. One may look in vain for a single word of his in any dictionary of quotations.

Long Melford ✤

It is worth the mile-long walk through the street at Long Melford just to see at close quarters the endless variety of styles and colours in the houses, the pubs and the shops, all in close proximity in this, the largest of our villages. As a reward for the effort there is the great church of High Trinity standing before you, magnificent in an oasis of green sward and with the beauty and proportions of a cathedral. Altogether it is 250 feet long and the tower, which is not part of the original building, is 180 feet high.

Inside the church is an unusual marble font and an alabaster relief of the Adoration of the Magi. There is a small chapel called the Clopton Chantry which was intended for prayers to be offered up for the souls of the Clopton family of Kentwell Hall. Much valued now for its graceful beauty and rich timber within is the annexe of the lady chapel. Former residents have not been so careful of this legacy for once it was used as a store room and later as a school. It consists of an inner chapel with enclosed 'cloisters' along the sides.

There are three great houses here all close by the village street. Melford Hall is a moated Tudor mansion with towers crowned with domes and with a garden that shows, with all else, the skill of the topiary artist. It was once the pleasure house of the abbot of Bury until such religious privileges were disposed of. Later it became the property of the Earls Rivers. It was the widow of the third earl who held the property when it was ransacked and plundered during the Civil War, the countess losing much of her fortune through the intrusion.

Kentwell Hall is another Elizabethan house with moat and bridges, the home once of the Clopton family. In recent years there has been a great project here to open the Hall to the public as an entirely Elizabethan concept, with food, music and costume to make this beautiful setting of Kentwell Hall as realistically Tudor as possible.

Also looking on to the village street is Melford Place, home of the ancient family of Martyns. The Martyns, Cloptons and the Cordells are all remembered here in the church. Sir William Cordell, who built the fine almshouses on the green, who welcomed Queen Elizabeth to the town and who held high office under both the Tudor queens, lies in an elaborate tomb with a marble canopy and

COTTAGES AT
LONG MELFORD.

106

with the Virtues of Prudence, Justice, Temperance and Fortitude watching over him.

Fairs were held here on the green on Whit Tuesday, Wednesday and Thursday, the first two days given to pleasure and pedlary, the last day for cattle. Silk weaving continued well into the last century, when there were three corn mills, six malting houses, a foundry, a rope manufacturer, a whitesmith, a tinner and two milliners.

Martlesham 🦋

This is where everything happens. The newspaper-cuttings file on Martlesham is bigger than that of any other village in the county. Great new projects have been opened up here, due partly to the varied and imaginative use of the war-time airfield and its buildings. Prominent, of course, is the Telecom research complex which the Queen opened in 1975. Here too is the Headquarters of the Suffolk Police.

Situated on the edge of the heath, the huge and extremely ugly Telecom building looks down like a Gulliver in Lilliput on scores of small business premises occupying old and new buildings where once the R.A.F. reigned supreme. The airfield — it was called an aerodrome before the Americans came — had a distinguished role in the last war as a fighter base and even before, when aeroplane flying was still in the developing stages. In 1940 I watched German bombs falling on Martlesham aerodrome in the early days before defences were properly organised. Later, such attacks were thwarted by early warning systems and increasing air strength.

Almost opposite the Telecom building a complete village has been created since the war. Individual styles of houses and varying situations, with plenty of space make this completely different from most housing estates.

All this belongs to the upper end of Martlesham before it dips down by the hill, quite steep for these parts, to the older half of the village in the valley of the Fynn. Almost at the end of its long journey through the countryside, the little river will join the Deben at the inlet known as Martlesham Creek. At the exact bottom of the hill is the well-known 16th century Red Lion inn, as popular with the users of the busy A12 as with coaching travellers of the past. A fearsome red ship's figure-head on the inn is believed to have come from a ship wrecked off the Suffolk coast but the origin is not certain and the long-standing controversy raises an added interest in the Red Lion.

The church, fittingly, hides itself demurely in the old part of the village in a quiet side-road. The tower is well patterned with Suffolk flints and inside there is a Jacobean pulpit and a huge, ancient chest.

Mellis

Mellis gives the visitor plenty of room to breathe, for here is one of the largest open commons in the county, probably a mile long altogether. It is a refreshing change from narrow lanes to be confronted by this vast expanse of rough grass on which a few tethered animals graze and wandering fowls and geese are almost lost to the view. The only sign of man's work on the common is the old well, covered with a roof and distinctly antique-looking nowadays though it has provided the water for nearby families for generations.

Looking on to this very pleasant rural prospect is a sprinkling of old-style houses including Mellis Hall, now a farmhouse. It was once the great manor-house called Pountney Hall, the seat of the Clarke family before it was largely demolished. On a corner of the common stands the very ancient church of St. Mary the Virgin, minus a tower which fell down in 1735. Although there was a public subscription at one time to rebuild the tower, it has never been accomplished and somehow the semi-ruin suits the sense of age and remoteness here. In the church there are memorials to the Clarkes and a tablet to a rector's daughter who lost her life while serving with the V.A.D. during the Great War.

There is also the tomb of Francis Yaxley, a diplomat of the 16th century and a 'foolish, prating knave' who was sent to the Tower for giving away State secrets. On his release, he went to Spain on behalf of Mary, Queen of Scots to ask for aid against Elizabeth. Facing almost certain death on his return for high treason, it was perhaps fortuitous that he was drowned on the voyage home.

Melton ❧

Melton joins itself equably to the town of Woodbridge without any noticeable break and then carries on along a fine, straight road to the village proper. It is at Melton's river bridge that we are allowed the first crossing of the Deben from its estuary at Felixstowe. Over Wilford Bridge lie the scenic areas of the Heritage Coast, stretching away up to Southwold and containing such a mixed bag of blessings as R.A.F. and U.S.A.F. air bases, a treasure trove (at Sutton Hoo), a nuclear power station (Sizewell) and a bird sanctuary (Minsmere). There is enough open space here, however, for the visitor to forget all these things and relax, have a quiet walk or a picnic among the bracken or on the edge of the forest areas.

The village of Melton keeps itself properly to its side of the bridge, nursing the beautiful church and the community centre which has recently been spared the trials of passing traffic by the introduction of a by-pass road. The elegant church spire looks down on a particularly handsome exterior (unfortunately locked) and a church-yard with nary a tombstone in sight. Instead, the church is surrounded by smooth, well-cut lawns and rose beds, the only monumental concession to the past being the two unobtrusive war memorials. A memorial of a different sort can be seen in one of the windows where the Victorian novelist, Henry Seton Merriman is given the importance his books once earned by their wide popularity. Merriman lived here and was only 41 when he died.

A mile or so along the old road to Wickham Market is the entrance to St. Audry's Hospital, once officially called the Suffolk Lunatic Asylum and in my young days simply the Melton Asylum. Unfortunately this was usually reduced further to 'Melton' so that a slight opprobrium attached itself to the place. I don't suppose it ever worried anyone then and certainly means nothing nowadays. St. Audry's was originally a House of Industry.

There was once a gaol here, notorious for the housing of religious dissentients at the time of Tudor persecution. Two of those unfortunates incarcerated while awaiting trial and inevitable death were Alice Driver and Alexander Gouche. Alice was a simple, forthright country girl who spoke her mind about the regime but when Alexander came hot-foot to Grundisburgh to warn her of her danger she agreed to hide with him in a stack of straw. Vicious, long

OLD ST. ANDREW'S CHURCH ~ MELTON ~ SUFFOLK.

hay forks soon forced them out and they were taken forthwith to
Melton gaol. At the trial, Alice, with stubborn honesty, said that she
considered Mary Tudor to be a Jezebel. For this remark her ears
were cut off before she was sentenced to death. Both she and
Alexander were burned at the stake at Ipswich.

Mendlesham

What was it that caused the creation of this very large and ancient
village in the first place? There are two quite long and closely-
packed streets of houses called Front Street and Old Market Street,
now designated a conservation area, and several small off-shoots.
The population was around 1500 in the 1851 census and before
that probably higher still. Yet there are no obvious reasons for a
large community to be situated here, away from main road and
river, without industry or railway. (There was a branch line here

between 1902 and 1953). Through the centuries the mainstay has undoubtedly been agriculture though some weaving was done and a regular market held at one time. There is a weaver's window in Front Street and a retting pit still discernible in a nearby field where flax was soaked before it was worked.

Mendlesham has that odd characteristic seen in one or two other villages round about, of having a major community in one place and a kind of satellite village a couple of miles away. In this case the lesser hamlet is called Mendlesham Green. At nearby Wetheringsett there is a similar arrangement with a separate unit two miles away. Here the smaller place is called Wetherup. One thing is certain, that wherever these twin communities occur there is very close rivalry, in the past often of a violent kind.

Situated at the base of both village streets is the beautiful church built on the site of an earlier Saxon church. The 13th, 14th, and 15th centuries all had a hand in the building. Among the remarkable objects to be found in the church is a font cover that reaches up in a great pyramid of magnificent style and decoration. It was made in 1630 by John Turner, a craftsman of Mendlesham. Another notable craftsman was Daniel Day, who in the 18th century had a workshop in Front Street where he produced the rare and latterly much-valued Mendlesham chairs. Two of the chairs can be seen beside the altar. John Knyvet, lord of the manor at the time that the church was built, is remembered in a brass portrait showing him in the armour of the period.

More exciting, and the object of many a visitor from far-off places is the priest's chamber. Here, up some steep stairs and within the well-guarded room is a rare collection of medieval and Tudor armour. There are 23 pieces altogether, including an Elizabethan long-bow. Among less war-like items are two standard pewter jugs used to check the measures in local inns and hostelries.

In the early days of television, the name of Mendlesham was familiar to everyone in the area as the site of the 1000-feet-high mast. It stands way out of the village and beside the main Ipswich to Norwich road, a spectacular addition to the rural scene that has caused many a motorist to risk trouble by craning his neck. Beneath the mast are the remains of the runways of the war-time airfield, once the base for bomber planes. Now, the hangars and other buildings have come into good use as warehouses and repositories of goods.

Mettingham 🌿

'You can't miss it' if you travel between Bungay and Beccles and you are bound to do this if you are in that great northern curve of the Waveney. Mettingham had a castle, square-built and powerful but used as a college for priests.

It was John de Norwich who decided that his mansion house should be turned into a real castle. As a gallant admiral of the king's fleet, he had some influence with Edward III and obtained the royal permission to do so. John then set about fortifying and extending his house until he had an immense, quadrangular structure but instead of filling it with men-at-arms as one might think, he brought priests and a master and installed them in the castle. There were 13 priests or chaplains and these provided the basis for a college for the training of young boys for the priesthood. The college was well-endowed from several manors round about.

John de Norwich died in 1363 and the ownership of the castle came down indirectly through several relatives to a young woman named Catherine de Brews. Catherine, however, was more concerned with spiritual wealth and renounced the inheritance to become a nun.

There are ruins still of the great gateway to the castle and indications that a moat and a wall surrounded the site.

Middleton 🌿

Here is an example of a Suffolk village which has completely disappeared. It was called Fordley and it stood beside Middleton on the heathland beside the little river Minsmere. Each village had a church but so close together they shared the same churchyard and a great deal of hostility grew up between the two parishes because of the sound of each other's church bells. If the times of the Sunday services were not synchronised, the congregation of one had to suffer interruption of their service by the noise. The two clergymen in office shared the animosity of their separate parishes and would make no effort to stop the nuisance. In the end, a petition was sent by church-goers to the Bishop of Norwich, who ordered that there should be one minister only and he should officiate at both churches

MIDDLETON

alternately. In those days, when every church had its parson, the judgment was regarded as being akin to Solomon's.

The identity of little Fordley soon began to disappear. The two parishes merged as Middleton-cum-Fordley although the church preferred Fordley-cum-Middleton because Fordley had a rectory and Middleton a vicarage. No doubt it seemed important once but now all references to Fordley and all traces of its church have gone. On the other hand, Middleton became a substantial community in the last century with a score of craftsmen including five shoemakers.

A separate part of the village is called Middleton Moor, and though this is an unusual term in Suffolk, the appearance of the windswept expanse of grass here proves that it is not badly named. The proximity of heathland always provides a certain air of desolation and this carries in to the very centre of this small community.

Monk Soham

Just outside the village proper is Hungers Green. It could, of course, refer to someone's name but if it means what it seems to mean it is in good company. In different parts of the county I have come across Hunger Hall (twice), Hungergut Hall, Starknaked Farm and Threadbare Hall. I have looked in vain for Abundance Hall or Repletion Hall.

Monk Soham, as the name suggests, was the resort of monks before the Reformation and whether they came for penance or for pleasure there is no doubt there was a constant interchange with the Abbey at Bury St. Edmunds. Fishing they certainly indulged in for the fishponds they used can still be identified. But, as with all such establishments, the heyday came to an end and Henry VIII gave the manor to Antony Rous who sold it to Lionel Tolmach soon after Elizabeth's accession.

The church contains many early treasures, with a font as old as the chancel itself and a Jacobean chair and magnificent iron-bound chest. It also has a sprinkling of monuments to devoted servants. Rectors had notoriously long lives even in the days when so many of the population died young. Here lived the longest of all, the Rev. F. Capper, credited with 59 years in the pulpit. Beside him, the incumbency of Fitzgerald's great friend Robert Groome of 44 years, seems moderate. Another rector stayed for half a century!

Nacton ⚜

It was a pleasant place for famous sea-dogs to retire to and it is still quiet and attractive, despite the new roads round about that are busy with the traffic to and from the port of Felixstowe. Here lived Broke of the Shannon, hero of the battle against the Chesapeake in 1813 and close by was the wealthy Vernon family whose admiral was the one who captured Porto Bello. The wooded slopes of their estates stretched side by side down to the foreshore of the river Orwell. They could have looked across the river to the villages of Pin Mill and Chelmondiston, while nowadays the view to the right shows the great curve of the Orwell Bridge, by no means unpleasant to look at and a fine achievement in traffic diversion from Ipswich.

Broke House had been built about 1767 though the family had lived there at what was called Cow Haugh since 1526 when Sir Richard Broke established the estate. Larger and more ostentatious was the home of the Vernons, the vast Orwell Park mansion that was built in the 18th century. The only other notable establishment along this stretch of the Orwell was Alnesbourne Priory, a cell of Augustinian monks attached to the abbey at Woodbridge. Later the priory became a farmhouse but the name remains. At a later period the Woodbridge Workhouse was sited at a spot called the Seven Hills, a seemly distance from the village proper. The 'hills' are believed to be barrows and the site of a great battle against the Danes in 1010.

For all the extent of the Broke and Vernon estates and the keepers paid to protect them, smuggling used to take place all along the river. The exploits of one of these smugglers and the Nacton servant girl unfortunate enough to fall in love with him form one of the best-known of Suffolk's stories. The account was written by the Rev. Richard Cobbold, whose mother employed Margaret Catchpole as a domestic servant and the book is basically true though embellished beyond credibility at some points.

Most people know the story of how this spirited girl was persuaded to steal a horse from her employer and ride it pell-mell to London to meet her lover, how she escaped from prison to meet him yet again and saw him shot down by her side and how at last she was deported to Australia. There she became an unofficial nurse to the settlers' families, became deeply interested in the country's affairs and sent back to England many of the examples of wild life that she discovered.

Margaret was a remarkable girl, even when setting aside her obsession for the smuggler, Will Laud. Youngest but one in a farm labourer's family of six children, she taught herself to read and write and at the age of thirteen showed herself capable of quick thought and action. She had been sent to a neighbouring farm with a message and on arrival there found the mistress in a fit and the servants standing around helplessly. Margaret immediately gave instructions to the servants, ran out to the yard and discovered the only horse, a young Punch with only a halter around its neck. In an instant she was galloping into Ipswich to fetch a doctor, without saddle or bridle, her clothes and hair flying. It was an event that had country people talking for long after and made the doctor an admiring friend of the young maid.

Nayland 🦋

This is another pearl in that beautiful necklace of villages that spreads itself along the north bank of the river Stour. It has been loved by many, including John Constable who painted the altar picture for the church of St. James. The picture is one of only two religious works that Constable painted, this his second and last.

At the height of the Suffolk weaving industry, Nayland was one of the most prosperous cloth-making centres – only Lavenham and Boxford produced more. The evidence of solid affluence over the centuries can be seen in the substantial, individually-styled houses and in the impressive size and elegance of the church. In 1552 there were 14 clothmakers, which is more important than it sounds, for they were the employers of weavers, fullers and shearmen. One well-to-do clothmaker named William Abell left his mark literally in the fabric of the village. Having built the single-span arched bridge across the Stour to Essex, he turned his attention to the church and constructed its most handsome porch. In it he proudly added·a simple logo of his name, a capital A within the shape of a bell.

Two guilds of weavers had their centre at the Guildhall which was substantial enough to survive the apprentices of the Middle Ages and then last through two centuries as a bakery before coming to rest, comparatively speaking, as an antique shop.

The splendid church was built about 1400 on the site of an even older church. A good deal of reconstruction has been done since, particularly in 1834 when the tower was replaced and a spire added to make it a superlative landmark in the district. Unwelcome attentions were paid at the time of the Civil War when a number of Roundheads destroyed 30 'superstitious pictures'.

There is a memorial to that distinguished churchman, musician and scientist, the Rev. William Jones, who became curate here in 1777. To his everlasting remorse, he was a distant member of the family of Oliver Cromwell, whom he despised. His brother-in-law had been one of the judges at the trial of Charles I and had suffered execution at the Restoration. In the eyes of the Rev. Jones this did not absolve his family's part in the death of the king and he felt the shame so acutely that each year he set aside the anniversary of that day as one of penance.

Needham Market 🌿

Ups and downs occur in all village histories in varying degrees; in the case of Needham Market there seems to have been a preponderance of misfortunes. To begin with, it is not very flattering to know that Needham (without the suffix) has always been simply 'a hamlet of Barking' or that, at one time, the signs of decay and desolation in the village were such that the simile 'as poor as Needham' became a common saying.

It was not always so. In the Middle Ages the place was busy and prosperous, with a considerable trade in woollen goods and a weekly market on Wednesdays. Each year in October there was a fair for cattle and general merchandise. But catastrophe arrived suddenly in 1685 when a revival of the plague struck the community. It brought an end to the good times, the market was abandoned and the production of woollens gradually lost to newer processes elsewhere. It was a long time before the village could re-establish itself but local agriculture, milling and a paper factory sustained the population over the difficult years. In 1793 a determined effort was made to recover lost prosperity by dredging the river Gipping, allowing barges to come up the river from Ipswich to the mill and beyond to Stowmarket.

Needham Market teeters on the brink of being a town and the extensive building projects all around have certainly boosted the population considerably though few of the newcomers have their work here. The long main street is closely built with houses and shops of all kinds, buildings that are ancient and varied but of no great distinction. The little church stands beside the houses in the street and though Kirby dismissed it as a 'mean building' it accords very well with the architecture about.

Newbourne 🌿

Newbourne lies exactly in the centre of the triangle formed by the towns of Ipswich, Woodbridge and Felixstowe. It is one of the few villages that can claim a complete transformation, thanks to the Land Settlement Association and the government policy between the wars of giving aid to unemployed miners. Until the time that researchers decided that Newbourne was ideal for settlement, it was no more than a mere hamlet. The church overlooked a few cottages and the Fox Inn from its raised situation among the trees and the old Hall nearby held nothing but its memories. The new 'settlement' changed it all.

It was a brave new scheme. Each 'settler' was provided with a 5-acre plot on which was a brand-new house, a range of piggeries and outbuildings and a large greenhouse. Assistance was given in the way of practical advice by experts and financial aid in the purchase of essential requirements like tools and fertilisers. There was also a well-planned organisation for collecting, transporting and marketing all produce from the holdings. It must have seemed a very strange environment to the families who had cut themselves off from their northern roots but most of them hung on through good times and bad and became part of the indigenous population – 'settlers' no more.

In the graveyard of the fine old 14th century church is the tombstone of the Suffolk Giant. It tells how the Giant travelled the country to be exhibited in sideshows, usually with his brother who was also of massive size. Little more is known of them though there have been fictionalised accounts of their lives.

Norton

'Yet I have heard,' wrote the ancient scribe, 'that there was a mine of Gold oare hereabouts (in Suffolk) but it is improbable hearsay.'

It was improbable then, even more so to us now, knowing that the centuries have not yielded anything more from the soil than the regular returns from tillage and that our gold and silver and copper too, all come out at the level of the price of corn and sugar-beet.

Yet the diggers came to Norton to seek out gold for their king, Henry VIII, he whose wealth seemed never to be enough to stop him itching for more. From some source or other the king believed that there was gold. No time was lost before sending men to explore the possibility by simple pick and shovel exploration. How exhaustive their activities were is unknown but records show that, perhaps from frustration, the excavations were not levelled but lay for a long time in heaps and holes. Whoever persuaded the king to do something so foolish probably had reason to regret doing so later.

There is no gold in the church either but there is much wealth in timber and stone and in the ancient craftsmanship visible all around. The church keeps its treasures modestly to itself aside from the main road that goes through the village to Ixworth and Thetford but it is worth the pause on a long journey to take a peep inside.

Offton 🌿

It seems an unlikely association at first glance – that of Offa, King of Mercia and this quiet village which seems to be far away from that monarch's territory. One generally assumes that Offa was pre-occupied with his Dyke and with events in the west of his region, yet the story is that he erected a castle here and gave his name to the community. Certainly there is still a mound of some size and a moat that seasonally fills up with water. Of building material there is no sign but this could be explained by the fact that such ruins were avidly plundered at one time for the repairing of roads.

Offton was large enough at the time of the Domesday Book to have two churches ascribed to it. The church that remains is plain and homely-looking, except for a handsome crown of battlements on the tower. There is an undecorated Norman door and a sober interior, perhaps due in some degree to the visits of William Dowsing. The floor was re-paved at the time of Victoria's Jubilee at the expense of the parishioners and as a lasting monument to the great Queen. On the font is a carving of the crown and crossed arrows that symbolise the martyrdom of Edmund. A monument of an unusual kind stands in the churchyard. It is of a horse standing very dejectedly over the supine figure of what seems to be a fallen rider.

Orford 🌿

The bonus for the traveller to Orford is that the whole journey from Melton onwards is through a beautiful countryside of forest and heath. With a score of roadside areas to stay and relax in, it is not a

STUBBLE FIELDS
NEAR OFFTON.

course to be rushed but rather to stay and smell the heather and the clean air from the sea. Then, quite contrary to Stevenson's dictum that it is better to travel hopefully than to arrive, the little town itself will welcome you with a charm all its own.

The castle is the great attraction, as it deserves to be, for this must be one of the finest and best-preserved keeps in the whole country. The 90 foot high fortified tower stands just beside the village centre on grassy undulations that still mark the ancient ditches and it looks out across the river to the marshes of Orfordness. Hugh Bigod and John Fitz-Robert were made governors of the castles of Norwich and Orford in 1215 and the responsibility was carried on to many shoulders until in recent times it came to the Marquis of Hertford and then to Lord Woodbridge, who gave it to the nation.

The castle, built in a polygon of 18 sides and flanked by three square towers, has walls that are 20 feet thick. At the base they are solid but higher up some small chambers and embrasures have been gouged out. Around the walls was a moat, then a bank with a 40 foot high wall and then another moat, all completely encircling the keep. Another feature discouraging to the unfriendly visitor was that the only access was made about 10 feet from the ground. Inside,

there are four rooms one above another and all connected by a spiral staircase of well-worn stone.

The castle was threatened with demolition in 1805 by the Marquis of Hertford until it was pointed out by coastguards that it was a valuable landmark for shipping. By keeping the castle in line with the church ships were assured that they were following a proper course that would avoid the dangerous Whiting sand-bank.

Seaward of the castle, the terrain is much affected by the odd behaviour of the river Alde which initially flows toward the sea but changes its mind at the last moment and turns south to run parallel to it. The peninsula so caused is almost entirely of mud and marsh. It makes a fine sanctuary for certain kinds of birds including the avocet, a few of which have commonly nested on the marshes of Halvergate Island.

Like other towns on our coast-line, Orford is much reduced from the glories of the past. It was once a port, busy with fishing and ship-building and in 1359 was able to send 3 warships and 62 men to assist in the siege of Calais. Orford was recognised as a borough and returned two Members to Parliament until the Reform Act of 1832. The town itself was governed by a mayor, 8 port-men, 12 burgesses and a recorder. There was a market every Monday and two annual fairs, with a court of sessions once a year.

Now, Orford is a very pleasant, small community with a partly ruined church near the open centre, a long, straight road down to the deserted quay and mud-bound river and the proud castle surveying all. When the wind blows in from the sea and sings in the marsh grass and sedges, it is easy to recall the legend of the monster, the Wild Man of Orford.

According to the ancient story, a sea monster in the form of a man covered in long hair was brought up in fishermen's nets close off shore in the reign of King John. The creature was taken to the governor of the castle who cared for it with great interest for some time. Apparently it fed upon fish or flesh, slept at sunset and rose at sunrise. A cage was constructed in the harbour so that the Wild Man could live in his own environment but it soon escaped. According to the story generally followed, it returned later and lived with the fishermen for a time before it disappeared forever.

Otley

Otley spreads itself comfortably in good farming country close to the ancient estate of the Tollemaches at Helmingham. It has its own handsome Tudor hall with bricks in herring-bone pattern between the beams, a house that once belonged to the Gosnold family but is no longer a private dwelling. John Gosnold, whose monument is in the church, was a country gentleman who showed an extraordinary personal loyalty to three successive sovereigns. No other man could ever have known more of the private lives of public monarchs and his knowledge all but cost him his head and certainly lost him his beloved home at Otley.

He was gentleman-usher at the court of Queen Elizabeth I until her death, when he transferred his duties to the new king from Scotland, James I. His services to the royal household must have been highly valued for when Charles became king, Gosnold was appointed a gentleman of the Privy Chamber. Someone so close to the king could not hope to escape when the king was beheaded and punishment came in the shape of heavy fines, so harsh that the estate at Otley had to be sold.

Another name remembered in the church is that of Samuel

Rogers, believed to be the longest serving of all the long-serving rectors of Suffolk, with a record of 67 years. Since the last war, Otley has become widely known for the Agricultural Centre here where a great deal of experimental and educational work goes on for the benefit of the farming industry.

Oulton 🌿

This is the gateway to the Broads, a place for summer leisure and holiday indolence, standing between Lake Lothing to the east and the expansive Broad to the west. Boating in one form or another is the entire, absorbing commitment of the village, its *raison d'etre*. Those who are not actually afloat are doing something to boats or watching those who are doing something to boats. Not many, perhaps, will have time to stare at the ancient church beside the water or to stay to pay homage to that grandiose character, Sir John Fastolfe who lies here. The old warrior had fought in France, enjoying the victory at Agincourt but suffering defeat at the hand of the Maid of Orleans and he had returned here to be caught and immortalised as Falstaff in the plays of Shakespeare. It is a character largely of the dramatist's fancy, of bluff soldier and comic figure together and somewhat larger than the real-life man, regarded by some as a ruthless mercenary.

There was at one time a brass in the chancel of the church showing Sir John and his wife Catherine in effigy, their feet resting on a greyhound. It was inscribed: 'John Fastolf, esquyer, died 1445 and Katern his wyef 1478.'

But if Fastolfe will not tempt the would-be sailors from their boats, there is another literary association that may well do so. George Borrow spent the last years of his life here within sight of the Broad and in his summer-house under the trees wrote his most memorable works – *Lavengro*, *The Bible in Spain* and *The Romany Rye*.

Borrow was born at East Dereham in Norfolk and much of his boyhood was spent in travelling from one place to another with his soldier father, Captain Borrow. Perhaps it was then that the lust for untrammelled wandering entered his blood but he dutifully followed his father's wish that he should become a lawyer and was articled to a solicitor in Norwich. How long he would have continued to do so, studying law and indulging his penchant for learning foreign languages, it is impossible to say, or how deeply unhappy he may have felt. But when his father died, he found the door to freedom was wide open and the fresh winds beckoning him out of doors. Borrow took to the open road where for long periods his only companions were gypsies and fair-ground prize-fighters. He learned the gypsy language and their customs and was accepted as one of their own kind. When he came back to live at Oulton, it was of gypsies and the wonder of open-air freedom that he wrote. He seemed to capture the very essence of that world in the words spoken by the gypsy Petulengro: 'There's day and night, brother, both sweet things; sun, moon and stars, brother, all sweet things; there's likewise a wind on the heath. Life is sweet, brother.'

Borrow kept all his love and admiration for simple people, welcomed them to his house and told them tales of the years he had spent wandering in Spain, sustaining himself by selling bibles. When he was alone he worked away in his solitary hut and only the humble and the down-trodden had the right to disturb him.

Palgrave 🐚

This is a charming Suffolk annexe to the Norfolk town of Diss. Separated only by the arbitrary line of the river Waveney, it enjoys a rural spaciousness that the town dwellers may envy. There is a large village green with an abundance of trees and a 14th century church whose Norman font is still in use. Several distinguished people have known Palgrave in the past, if only as boarders at the old grammar school where Chief Justice Lord Denman and Sir William Gill attended. The school mistress herself, Anne Letitia Barbould, was both disciplinarian and author, much admired in the literary world.

The most interesting character of the village was Thomas Martin, F.A.S. 'Honest Tom Martin' he was called and it was a cognomen of which he was very proud. He was born at Thetford in 1696, son of a rector there and seventh in a line of nine children. He attended the grammar school in the town of which he was later to write a history. With family inclinations toward the law, he became articled to his brother who was an attorney. Possible achievements in this direction were destined to be swamped by the effects of Thomas's two marriages – the first brought a large family and the second, to the widow of Peter De Neve, an immense amount of antiquarian treasure in the form of ancient manuscripts, prints and books.

As time went on, Thomas became more and more absorbed in the study, collecting and cataloguing of antiques until he seemed to lose sight of more practical matters. Every penny that he could afford went to buy additions to his collection until he was almost beggared amid all his wealth. When he died at the age of 75, he was alone and penniless but Honest Tom Martin was buried with honour in the porch of the church and an inscription placed above the spot.

Parham 🌿

To those of us around here in the war years, the name of Parham must always touch a chord of memory for it was one of the chain of airfields in the county and a prime base for bomber raids. Since then, the village has graciously accepted the mantle of peace and has benefited in rural charm through being off the main traffic routes and through having in its boundaries the calm spaciousness of open greens.

The Earls of Suffolk first held the lordship here and the second Earl built the church in the reign of Edward III. The Willoughby family came into possession through marriage and there was a succession of seventeen Lord Willoughbys before the title became extinct. Their home was Parham Hall, a double-moated Elizabethan mansion that is now a farmhouse. It was built on the site of a castle whose gateway, adorned with coats of arms, remained intact long after the main structure had fallen and was finally dismantled and taken to America.

Despite the depredations of William Dowsing who destroyed everything that looked 'superstitious' or 'popish', the church reveals a mass of interesting features including a font and a delicately-carved screen that are as old as the church itself.

George Crabbe, the rural poet, knew Parham well. He came here in good times and bad in his persistent wooing of Sarah Elmy, a niece of John Lovell who was a well-to-do yeoman of the village. A piece of local folk-lore that seems to give great satisfaction to some relates to the Parham thorn bush that is said to blossom at Christmas as well as at the normal season, thus rivalling the famous thorn at Glastonbury.

Peasenhall 🌿

This is a real old-timer of a village, large enough to have a street that is long and continuous, though nicely higgledy-piggledy. It is a place that tells of crafts and skilled, busy men serving the needs of the rural hinterland. Even now can be heard – or is it just my fancy? – the sound of hammer and plane if not the blacksmith's anvil. Why the community settled here and how it managed to survive must rest simply on local agriculture and the industry of craftsmen. Here in Peasenhall the farmers and their workers as well as the gentry could always obtain the basic goods and services that made life tolerable.

At about the time of Queen Victoria's accession the list of craftsmen was at its peak. Three blacksmiths, including a father and son kept the sparks flying at the forges while the same number of shoemakers, one of them a woman, busied themselves at the task of keeping feet dry and comfortable. There were three wheelwrights working, a saddler and collar maker, a cooper and a bricklayer, two carpenters and a plumber and glazier. In business there was a corn merchant and an enterprising family turning out seed and manure drills. Carriers plied regularly between Peasenhall and Norwich, Ipswich and Colchester. It was a hive of industry and not at all a likely setting for the murder that was to take place at the turn of the century.

This celebrated case, like that at Polstead Red Barn, concerned the murder of a young village servant girl, Rose Harsent. Suspicion settled upon William Gardiner, a business man and a pillar of the local Methodist church. At the trial, one juror prevented a unanimous verdict of guilty and a re-trial was ordered. Again the jury disagreed and Gardiner was acquitted. General belief, then and since concludes that he was guilty but escaped justice by the bungling of the prosecution and the use of a very aggressive barrister on his behalf. Certainly Gardiner did not stay to test local opinion – he immediately shaved off his beard and left the village for good.

Pin Mill 🌿

There are sailors that must go down to the sea again and those who prefer to stay in the river. At Pin Mill there is an abundance of the

latter kind, forming a considerable fleet of small leisure craft that threatens to over-flow into the neighbouring marina at Wollverstone. Besides its small, modern boats, Pin Mill is also renowned for its tradition of barge sailing. The Pin Mill Barge Match was held each year on a Saturday in July when stout old vessels of long service would sail to the estuary and back. It was a silent, graceful and yet still supremely exciting competition and people lined the shores of the Orwell to watch. On such occasions, as on others, the Butt and Oyster, whose hallowed beams date so far back as 1500, would become a centre of activity and the scene of endless swapped yarns of river men. In the days when young boys were trained for the Navy at H.M.S. Ganges at Shotley, they too would find their way to Pin Mill to join the common interest.

The name of the village has aroused much speculation in the past. One school of thought seems to believe that it simply comes from the term 'pin money'. Apparently, when a local *grande dame* named Elizabeth Woolverston died, a list of her possessions included two mills on the banks of the Orwell, given to her by her father as 'pin money'. A more erudite line is that the name comes from 'pynd' or 'pennd' which in early English described a mill pond of fresh water.

Many illustrious barges have sailed from here, none more worthy than the old *Tollesbury* that made the Little Ships journey to Dunkirk in 1940 and rescued nearly 400 tired soldiers from the beaches. Local sailors remember the disasters of the war and the

127

floods of 1953 as almost synonymous. The floods could be foreseen, they say, and were predicted before any official warnings were given. At Pin Mill the awesome combination of wind and tide caused the water to advance at a rate that would overtake a running man. As it happened, many people here were in the best place, living on houseboats that rose with the tide.

At the end of the war, when many countries felt that they owed a debt of gratitude to Britain, the Swedish radio broadcast a programme on Suffolk and Pin Mill in particular, pointing out the individual sacrifices it had made for victory. It ended: 'The county of Suffolk was foremost in volunteer work in the war. It was first in England to get out a survey of its population resources and industry for post-war planned development. It was the first to prepare its post-war scheme for the expansion of water and electricity supplies to country districts. The village of Pin Mill, which was steadfast in war, is also determined to be in the vanguard of progress in peace.'

Playford ✑

The message that Playford gives out is that it is not just a pretty place, though that is true enough. Unlike many villages that keep themselves very much to themselves, Playford offers any visitor who has two feet and is willing to use them a chance to become better acquainted.

It has been a great delight of mine for many years to take advantage of this opportunity. There are footpaths here through beautiful countryside in all directions. A favourite of mine is to follow the course of the Fynn to Aldercarr or alternatively to take the Warren Path past the woods to Donkey Lane. There is a maze of paths here, many of them beckoning towards the neighbouring village of Tuddenham. What could be better than to come out at last beside the Fountain Inn? If ever you tire of walking in that direction you can go by the quiet back road past the high-banked church that is mantled in trees and try the Squeech Path into Pigs Valley, where you will find no pigs but a plantation of rustling poplars. The wonder is that so few ever set foot in these delightful ways into the rural heartland. When the traffic is steaming and hissing on the main roads, here is a retreat, a solace that is never valued enough. If use is not made of footpaths, they will not remain open.

Playford Hall was for long the seat of the powerful family of Fultons but the most notable occupant of the mansion arrived after the Fulton line had become extinct. His name was Thomas Clarkson and he lived there for thirty years. An obelisk in the churchyard pays tribute to this man whose modesty has kept him almost unknown among the great reformers.

Thomas Clarkson, a schoolmaster's son destined for the church, became an M.A. of Cambridge and in the course of his final examinations wrote a thesis on human slavery. His studies and self-searching brought him to believe that this must be one of the most enormous sins of mankind. He felt that he could no longer accept a place on the sidelines while such a commerce in human freedom was taking place and instead of entering the Church, he thenceforward devoted his entire life to the fight for abolition.

His energy was unremitting. Wherever in Britain there were merchants, ship owners or profiteers engaged in the trade, there he would carry his crusade. Every port and any suspicious-looking ship came under his investigation and he wrote unceasingly on the injustice of the commerce. As his influence extended, he travelled to France and Russia to assist in their campaigns for the same cause. He lived to hear of the Emancipation Act which freed the slaves of the West Indies and to know that everywhere there was a new awakening of conscience about slavery of all kinds. He came back to Playford to spend the last years of his long life in this peaceful village.

Polstead ✤

There are so many attractive aspects to Polstead – the Pond or Pool place – it seems a pity that most visitors come only because of a crime committed here a century and a half ago. The Murder in the Red Barn has since been celebrated widely in story and melodrama. Even now, when violence becomes more frequent and more bizarre, the fascination of the story remains. The Red Barn was burned down long ago and the tombstone marking Maria Marten's grave has been despoiled and broken away to nothing. Only the cottage remains that housed the poor girl.

Perhaps only the story of Margaret Catchpole is known better in Suffolk. It is a drama with perfect ingredients to arouse emotions. A simple village maiden is wronged – as they used to say – by a villanous squire and innocent trust is spurned by upper-class sophistication. How many tears have been shed over this melodrama! Even after William Corder had been hanged for his crime, audiences booed and hissed at the make-believe character on the stage.

Polstead's beautiful church of St. Mary was built around 1160, when Henry II was king and Archbishop Thomas had a precious few more years before his murder in the cathedral. There have been some alterations but the Norman characteristics are there for all to see. In the 14th century a tower was added and later still a spire was placed on top of the tower, the only surviving stone spire in the county.

Almost as revered as the church was the Gospel Oak that stood close by until its final collapse in 1953. Religious ceremonies of some sort are believed to have been held here for hundreds of years and were revived some time ago in the form of an annual church service at the height of summer. There is a painting in the church of the oak as it was 100 years ago but there is no evidence that it was of such an age as some people have asserted.

In this attractive valley of the river Box the village of Polstead has added its own kind of beauty in the spring when acres of cherry trees have blossomed as a prelude to the crop of famous black cherries. Appreciative new villagers have raised the community awareness of the charms of the environment and work hard to keep all in good order. In the church yard, stones have been levelled and rose bushes planted by bereaved relatives of the dead. It all looks very tidy and it helps the grass-cutting, they say. One lady said she hoped that the churchyard turf would become as smooth as any Cambridge lawn.

Well, it is some sort of achievement. But I wonder if the time will come when we will search – as we already do for old objects, old places, old innocence – for an old-fashioned churchyard with its gravestones all awry and half-hidden in ox-eye daisies and buttercups. Tidiness is not all nor is practical expediency the final answer.

Rattlesden

Rattlesden is a place that asks to be visited simply for the old-world charm that still exists, a quality well assessed and much approved of by the newcomers who have settled here. It is a large and open village with several greens or commons and picturesque houses, a place where one can rest and forget the rest of the world. The only spectacular feature, which some older villagers deprecate as being unsuitable, is the pair of huge whalebones erected into a pointed arch near the bridge. Close observation of the changing condition of the bones has convinced at least one local man that it is possible to foretell the weather from them.

The village stands at one of the sources of the river Gipping and once received barges here that had sailed all the way from Ipswich. The Port of Bury St. Edmunds, it has been called, though people would probably smile at the description nowadays. Stone for the cathedral was brought here by boat and in later centuries so was contraband. From this point goods legal and illegal were put on to carts and carried overland. Such activity at the riverside is difficult to imagine now, for the tributary of the Rat is not much more than a good-sized ditch. A few years ago a great controversy grew up locally when it was suggested that the name Rat should be changed. Happily, it is still the Rat and the stalwarts who opposed the change can sleep peacefully until the next village crisis.

The church is believed to have been founded by the monks of Bury. It contains some fine carved screens and monuments to long-serving incumbents, one of them a rector for 53 years. An earlier rector seems to be here still in spirit for a spectre has been seen several times on the site of the old rectory and the story is that he was bricked up in the pantry to escape his debts, apparently with unfortunate results.

Redgrave ✤

For much of the past, particularly in the 18th and 19th centuries, the village has been dominated by Redgrave Hall, whose estate was once something like 20,000 acres and no doubt the employer of most of the peasantry. The lordship of Redgrave was first given to the abbey of Bury by Ulfketel, Earl of the East Angles, who was killed in 1016 in a battle against the Danes. At the Dissolution of the Monasteries, Henry VIII gave the manor to Thomas Darcy from whom it passed to the Bacon family, whose power and influence is recorded in many village histories.

The Hall was built by Sampson, Abbot of Bury, in 1211, the monks making use of the land for farming and the building as a spiritual retreat. Under the ownership of the Bacon and then the Holt families, the Hall and its territory became of baronial proportions although, when Queen Elizabeth visited in 1577, she thought it rather small. In or about 1770, the lord of the manor at that time, Rowland Holt, rebuilt the house and spent a fortune on improving the immediate landscape. In the great park were gardens laid out by Capability Brown and an immense lake of 45 acres. The estate came to be acknowledged as one of the foremost in the county.

Rowland Holt also paid for substantial restructuring of the church, including a new tower built of Woolpit bricks. It is a church that is naturally much given to remembering the great families here and the most spectacular of the monuments is the altar tomb of Sir Nicholas Bacon and his wife, Lady Anne, in black and white marble. Marble is used in other situations with great effect as it seems to attain a special beauty in this light and spacious church. Among the rectors here was one Thomas Wolsey, instituted in 1506, an ambitious churchman who was to become a Cardinal.

The Redgrave of today makes a charming picture with its open green and roadside pond in the centre. It also possesses a natural phenomenon that must be unique. Nearby are the sources of both the Waveney and the Little Ouse, each arising from a spring and each going in the opposite direction to the other. On the map it looks the same river, the border between Suffolk and Norfolk, but here is the unexpected truth. The Waveney flows eastwards and the Little Ouse westwards and both have their origin here.

Redgrave Fen, together with Lopham Fen, now comes under the control of the Suffolk Trust for the Conservation of Nature and is an area of great interest because of the variety of wild-life. Sedge, marsh and reed warblers are seen here with blackcaps and bearded tits while beneath the feet are many other natural denizens of the marsh, including adders, lizards and toads.

Rendlesham

It is odd that this tiny village, scattered and insignificant as it seems, should contain both the most ancient and the most modern features of the county. On its doorstep and encroaching into the forest and heath is the extensive American air-base of Bentwaters, from which the most up-to-date aircraft indulge in frequent and occasionally ear-splitting exercises. The adjacent forest, too, is shown to be out-of-bounds to the casual visitor. One young villager with pronounced sci-fi interests declared to me that strange things had happened thereabouts and he was convinced that a flying saucer had landed in the forest and the American authorities knew about it.

By contrast, Rendlesham is known to have been the seat of the ancient kings of East Anglia and took its name from one of them named Rendilus. The original name was Rendilisham which, as Bede says, means 'the house of Rendilus'. Redwald, another king of the East Angles, kept his court here at a palace of significant size. He was the first East Anglian to be baptized and to receive the faith of Christianity. It seems certain that an ancient silver crown was once dug up here. It weighed 60 ounces and was probably melted down.

Rendlesham House was built close by the site of the palace of the Angles in the Tudor period. It eventually came into the hands of Mr. P. J. Thelluson, who bought the estate for £51,400 and took the title of Lord Rendlesham when created a peer in 1806. During his lifetime the mansion was extended and improved, becoming what was described as 'a princely residence'. Certainly many members of royal and noble families visited there in the last century. Still visible to the many passers-by to the air-base is the spectacular but desolate-looking gateway, built by Lord Rendlesham in a Gothic style with some of the ruins of Butley abbey.

Rickinghall

Whether Inferior or Superior, it comes to much the same thing – a long straight street which they share with Botesdale. Where each begins and ends is a matter for the local purist as there is no obvious dividing line. The street on which they all stand is the old coaching route between Norwich and Bury St. Edmunds and somehow it seems a little bemused still by the activity of the present day.

Rickinghall Inferior has a round Norman tower to its church which is on the site of an earlier Saxon building. Additions were made to the church in the 13th and 15th centuries with a porch and a priest's room above. The colourful east window remembers the daughter of a Victorian rector, a popular girl who went happily on her honeymoon to Switzerland in 1870. By a tragic accident she fell into a crevasse and her body was never recovered.

The beautiful church of Rickinghall Superior dates from the 14th century. There is still a stone stairway to a room over the porch and a continuous stone seat on both sides of the nave. The lordship of the Rickinghalls was given to the monks of Bury by the Earl of East Anglia, Ulfketel. Henry VIII granted it to Nicholas Bacon with other lordships in the area and it was then bought by the Holt family. Sir John Holt was Lord Chief Justice and in his long career achieved a reputation for wisdom and tolerance, much needed in the days of witch-hunting and religious cruelty.

Rushbrooke 🪶

The propensity of a certain monarch for sleeping in other peoples' houses is clearly shown in the list of Suffolk mansions so honoured. 'Queen Elizabeth slept here' brings an added respect for the edifice and even more for the bed-chamber. When the queen made her celebrated progress through the county in 1578 with a royal entourage large enough to cause many a headache in Tudor kitchens, it was an occasion for great self-aggrandizement in the homes of the mighty though mixed no doubt with some trepidation. Her arrival at Rushbrooke Hall was the highest and most successful point of her journey, where joy was unconfined. With a suitable number of servants, equerries, court officials and ladies-in-waiting, the queen held her court here in the great drawing-room. Her host, Sir Robert Jermyn, provided sumptuous hospitality with much feasting and general merriment. French ambassadors were received here and entertained 'two several times, with which charges and courtesy they were wonderfully satisfied.'

The Jermyns had held the lordship since the Dissolution deprived the Abbey of Bury of its ownership. The Hall, situated in a beautiful park, was moated and formed a noble mansion on three sides of a square. At the time of the queen's visit there was a chapel which she used. Much of the furniture prominent at her receptions, together with bed hangings and other objects have been carefully preserved.

The village is only three miles south-east of Bury St. Edmunds and sits on one side of the river Lark. The 14th century church contains several monuments to the Jermyns, one of them a marble effigy of a young boy of 15, Thomas Jermyn, who was killed at that age by a falling mast.

Rushmere St. Andrew

Once a respectable amount of open space separated the village from Ipswich; now, part of it is already absorbed into the general plan of the town. However, all is not lost, by any means. There is still a good slice of heathland belonging to the villagers and, away from the busy main roads, the village image is desperately maintained. The quiet road that runs by the church is perhaps a little self-consciously rural, with real hedges and trees, an authentic pond and authentic, well-behaved ducks. But there are no authentic peasants sucking on straws.

The handsome church shows relics of the Norman period but much has been added through the centuries. The tower was built in the 16th century at the expense of Catherine Cayde, who expressed the wish that the Rushmere tower would be 'a steeple of like fashion, bigness and workmanship with that of Tuddenham.' The church at Tuddenham scores, of course, from being planted in a very impressive position on a hill close beside the village street, while Rushmere church is quietly ensconced in trees. There is a small stone statue of St. Andrew, the saint of the village, outside the west window.

The lordship belonged to William de Freney in the reign of King John, for there is a record of him paying fines at Ipswich on behalf of his villeins. Later, it came into the possession of the wealthy Feltons of Playford and thence passed to the Earl of Bristol. The hamlet of Bixley, once a separate parish, has been largely absorbed by the borough.

The situation of the village on the edge of a large town with an open expanse of common at its disposal, has not always been a boon. In these days the heath is given over chiefly to the golf course and the walking of dogs but local pastimes have not always been so innocent. Public hangings drew huge crowds in the 18th century and Rushmere had the space to entertain a concourse of spectators. The *Ipswich Journal* of April 10th 1790 has this paragraph: 'Three men have been executed at Rushmere in the presence of a great crowd of people. The men spoke soberly and all behaved in a penitent manner. The one named Mills addressed the crowd and exhorted them to take warning from their condition. Then they joined hands and were launched into eternity.'

One man whose career was brought to an end here on Rushmere Heath was John Hodgson, aged 26. This character was much given to serving in the armed forces and he had enlisted 98 times, sadly for personal rather than patriotic reasons. Each enlistment brought bounty money and in a few years he had amassed several hundred pounds. At each occasion he served his country for only a few hours, the longest spell being 48 hours. As the army business became more hazardous, John turned to work as a highwayman and it was for these activities that he was hanged.

Sibton ❧

Some villages have frank, open faces in which nothing is hidden from the curious glance. Others have their faces veiled or averted. Some, as at Sibton, are forever slipping out of sight altogether. Here, the few houses are far apart and the moment you think that you have reached the core of the village it disappears and you find yourself once more on the wrong road and somehow feeling rather cheated. 'To Sibton' the signpost says on the A12 near Yoxford; when you follow the road the only definite object you come across then is another signpost that points the way you have come and proclaims the same message – 'To Sibton'.

There are a few signs here still of the ancient abbey founded in 1149 for the monks of the Cistercian order. Apparently it was a very active and prosperous community, well-endowed by the wealthy. It came into the possession of the Duke of Norfolk and much later when the walls began to crumble the material was used to help build Abbey House nearby. The fishpond that the monks used to provide themselves with fresh fish can still be discerned. At the church entrance is a beautiful thatched lych-gate which is a memorial to the fallen in the Great War. A Norman doorway within a porch built 800 years later introduces the church interior with its richly decorated font and Jacobean pulpit. In the churchyard is a stone that tells us:

> 'The world's a city full of crooked streets,
>   And Death's a Market Place where all may meet.

If Life were merchandise that men could buy,
Rich men would live and only poor men die.'

The sentiment seems trite enough in the modern world but when written was probably a challenging and risky thing to say. Perhaps that is why the author had first placed himself out of reach of any reproof or reprisal.

Snape

It is an astonishing thing to come across this collection of maltings, unmarked save for a single sign on the country road, and reflect that this is a place famed for music perhaps the world over. Music, opera, virtuosi in the midst of these familiar sugar-beet fields? Who could have imagined such a thing? The buildings, the village and the river look much as they did when I used to watch the men shovelling the barley on the maltings floor. There is very little to indicate that anything but shovelling barley takes place here now. To be sure, there is a decorous art and craft shop hidden away somewhere and the ground is thick with visitors who come to stare and go away again but of modern bally-hoo there is none. You will get no more amusement than walking the river bank or patting the horse that looks out of the stable door. Yet of course, the maltings have to be visited. They have the magic of great names.

There is another name beside those of artists and musicians which is important in the history of the place – Garrett of Leiston. People of my generation will recognise it at once if they are natives of Suffolk for it was on the front of those lovable, trundling old steam-rollers and on the side of throbbing threshing machines and a host of other heavy engines. When I was a child it was the first name I learned to spell.

At the Garrett engineering works at Leiston, two brothers took over the business started by their father. Later, they separated, Richard the elder remaining in charge of the works while Newson took over the maltings at Snape. Newson Garrett gradually extended the buildings there until there was seven acres of malting floor space. He was something of an eccentric and it is said that he would mark out a new building simply by drawing his stick along

SNAPE MALTINGS
CONCERT HALL
SUFFOLK.

the ground. As he did not walk straight the main building still has a slightly bowed front.

At the height of the Garrett business the Alde was a busy highway. There were twelve ships plying for Newson and as many bringing in iron ore for Richard. The small quay beside the maltings was the furthest point to which a vessel could navigate and the bridge that carries the road is the first place from its estuary that the river can be crossed.

Newson Garrett died at the age of 82, leaving behind a large family brought up in the same mould of self-dependent endeavour as their father. Most famous of them was his favourite daughter Elizabeth, who as Elizabeth Garrett Anderson, became the country's first woman doctor and the first woman mayor.

Later generations of Garretts continued at the maltings but the heyday of malting was over. In the 1960s local maltings were being closed all over the country. At Snape the wooden shovels were put away forever in 1965. By chance the Aldeburgh Festival Committee was then looking for a permanent home and the brilliant idea of using the maltings was mooted.

The story of the courage and enterprise in transforming the old maltings is well known. The triumph was shared by many who knew or cared little for music but who admired the determination of those who were so dedicated. When, soon after all was completed, fire completely gutted the concert hall there was a groan of sympathy from one end of the country to the other.

The village of Snape does have a life of its own beside the Maltings though you would never guess it. To the stranger Snape means the Maltings — the Maltings means Snape. There's no mistake. You can't miss it.

Somerleyton 🌿

Like the whimsical river Alde further south, the Waveney shows a wilful nature when it approaches the sea. Almost within sight of it at Lowestoft, it then turns pettishly north-west and after losing itself in Breydon Water comes out finally at Yarmouth. It creates what is virtually an island here in the north-east corner of the county, in the centre of which is the village of Somerleyton.

The reputation of lordly splendour here comes chiefly from the famous Hall, now largely Victorian but still gracious and magnificent. It is set in the beautiful park of which Fuller once said – 'Sommerley Park is well named for here Summer is to be seen in the depth of winter in the pleasant walks on both sides, with fir trees green all the year long.'

The manor once belonged to the powerful Fitz Osbert family but when Sir Walter Jernegan married the daughter and heiress of Sir Peter Fitz Osbert, the manor came into his keeping. It was Sir John Jernegan who built the splendid Elizabethan hall. In the church are many memorials to those distinguished families of Somerleyton's past – the Fitz Osberts, Jernegans, Wentworths and Garneys. One is in the form of an altar tomb of Sir Thomas Jernegan, which once held the inscription:

'Jesus Christ, both God and man,
Save thy servant Gernegan.'

It was Sir Samuel Morton Peto, made wealthy by the railway boom, who made spectacular changes to the village during his occupation of the Hall. Apparently a man of great energy and spirit, he constructed what came to be known as a model village around the green with a natural style of building that blended well with the rural scene. He then practically rebuilt the Hall and restored the church.

This may be Suffolk's forgotten corner so far as many are concerned but crowds of people make their way here in the summer months to view the grandness of the Hall and the spaciousness of the park. There are magnificent trees here and a variety of types of ecology, with soils ranging from unproductive sand to unproductive marsh but with much good arable land between, some of it reclaimed from peat and clay. The farming is mixed, with stock and farm crops inter-grown with vegetables.

Not far away is the very popular stretch of water known as Fritton Lake and believed to be the most beautiful lake in East Anglia, lined as it is with woods and gardens. Along the two-mile stretch can be found recreations and diversions of all kinds.

Sotterley

Here is another village slightly reminiscent of feudal days, for the Hall and the great park have obviously dominated the quiet community in the past. Houses are scattered along the fringe of the estate which was once, no doubt, the centre of the universe for unlettered village labourers. So far as rural beauty goes, their lives could not have fallen in more pleasant places. The park itself, with a stream that swells to a lake in a setting of beautiful trees, covers something like 500 acres and also contains the 15th century church of St. Margaret, lofty and embattled.

The most prominent family to have lived here was the Playters, who held the manor as long ago as the reign of Edward II and continued in the village for over two hundred years. One of the Playters was created a baronet in 1623 but the title afterwards became extinct.

As expected, the church is a museum of Playter associations, the earliest being a brass of a 15th century Sir Thomas wearing armour of the time of the Wars of the Roses. A later Thomas figures in an impressive wall monument showing him on his knees but slightly above the effigies of his two wives. In a fine profusion underneath in carved relief are 21 children, the product of his two marriages.

The Southelmhams

The mother-hen of Southelmham sits on a clutch of six small villages in a very big backyard. Within the triangle of the towns of Harleston, Bungay and Halesworth a vast portion of the countryside is covered by the Southelmhams, whose total area must be counted in square miles. There are six separate communities, though community is perhaps not a word to use in this scattered area and each is named after a saint. In descending importance they are: All Saints and St. Nicholas, St. Cross or St. George, St. James, St. Margaret, St. Michael and St. Peter.

The whole area of the Southelmhams is completely agricultural and deeply rural. There is an atmosphere of past times in these villages that fits well with the sparse habitation. It is the kind of place that takes me back in memory to the country life of the twenties and thirties. Though I saw no working horses, here were old implements and odds and ends lying around in the casual fashion of farming before it was all tidied up. There was evidence too, of what was once the farmers's greatest skill – improvisation.

The largest of the Southelmhams is All Saints and St. Nicholas. Once they were separate parishes but the church of St. Nicholas fell into ruins and was never rebuilt. Now All Saints with its round flint tower caters for both and St Nicholas is remembered only by a lonely cross in a field.

St. Cross is large in area but very scarce in houses, with a small church which was repaired and re-pewed in 1841 to provide more sittings. Nearby a few ruins are left of an earlier church built in the 7th century.

St. James is another straggling village that includes an area of arable land named St. James' Park. This was once the site of the palace and demesne of the bishops of Norwich. During the 12th and 13th centuries it was a venue of great splendour visited by the high lights of the church and particularly at the time of Bishop Suffield's influence with the Pope.

St. Margaret. A smaller village, this, with hardly enough local inhabitants to keep the place warm.

St. Michael is even less populous – but it apparently holds on to what few it has. Eleven men went to serve in minesweepers in the war and all came back. Very few villages have this record.

At St. Peter there is an ancient hall, now a farmhouse, which was the home of the wealthy Tasburgh family in days gone by.

Stanton

Going into Stanton from the direction of Ixworth, I had the opportunity for a few words with one or two people fortunate enough to live in this very pleasant community. The first man I spoke to was a stranger, I suspected, missing the signs of the dedicated countryman. He had been here for eighteen years, he told me. Well, as I thought, a complete stranger. A more aged gentleman treated me to some reminiscences in slow, familiar Suffolk speech, 'I'm glad you still use the dialect,' I told him. He looked blank. 'What dialect?' he said.

A handful of Stanton building workers were repairing a barn here about a hundred years ago, and, perhaps feeling that the Queen's Jubilee required some special mark in history, wrote a patriotic message and placed it in a bottle which was hidden under the barn floor. The message, which was unearthed in 1948, said: 'This barn was repaired by Sturgeon Brothers but 65 years ago it was used as a Weslen Chapel: the part ware the bottle will be found was the door ware they went in.

Theair will be grate rejoicing in England this year as it is the Jubilee year of Hear Majesty reign Queen Victoria. H. S. Dudding is the rector of this parish but the parish is to poor to do enney thing for the Jubilee but they are trying to get an organ for the church which will cost £120.' Several names are added at the conclusion of the message together with the words – 'God Save the Queen.'

Once there were two separate parishes here of All Saints and St. John, but the latter church long ago fell into ruins and the village is consolidated into one. The manor was given to the abbey at Bury by Edward the Confessor and granted after the Dissolution of the Monasteries to Sir Thomas Jermyn. The village had the right of a fair on Whit Monday and May 12th for the purpose of 'pleasure and pedlery.'

Stoke-by-Clare ✿

This is another of those attractive villages that lie beside the river Stour. It is celebrated as the home of an archbishop and of a miser. Both these men were at some time associated with the college which developed from an early Benedictine priory. The college was installed with a dean and six canons and the last dean before the Tudor purge was the famous reformer and churchman Matthew Parker, who became Archbishop of Canterbury in the reign of Elizabeth.

In the 17th century the college property together with the manor came into the possession of Sir Gervaise Elwes, who was created a baronet in 1660. The title came to the grandson, Sir Hervey Elwes, with an inheritance of widespread debts. With a dedication that became an obsession, Sir Hervey swore that he would repay all his grandfather's debts even if it took a lifetime. In fact, it did not require so long a period. When he died at the age of 80, he had not only satisfied all creditors but had saved a fortune of £100,000. To achieve this, he had embarked on a policy of abstinence which has earned him lasting renown as a miser.

When he died the title became extinct and the fortune was inherited by his nephew, John Meggott, who changed his name to Elwes as required by the will. While Sir Hervey had had some excuse for his miserliness, his nephew had none but soon proved that he could out-do his uncle at parsimony. The mansion fell into ruins for want of repairs while John would be out in the fields to glean a little corn or to find a few sticks. Or he would be in the greenhouse seeking to catch the free warmth from the sun, since he would have no fire until the coldest weather. Perhaps there is some mitigation even of his scale of penny-pinching for he had been well schooled in the science in his early life when his mother, with a fortune of £100,000 to hand, starved herself to death.

Stoke-by-Nayland

About six miles from Hadleigh and just north of Nayland itself is one of our most illustrious villages. The church alone proclaims the fact to anyone who doubts it. The commanding tower with its triumphant corner pinnacles rises 120 feet into the sky and can be seen in all its glory from far and wide. It looks down on a nave and chancel of Tudor splendour. About the church is a cluster of fine timbered houses.

There are two mansions hereabouts with histories of distinguished occupants. Gifford's Hall, in ancient times the seat of the Giffords, came to the Mannock Family in the reign of Henry IV and a long succession of Mannocks have followed. Within the church are many memorials to the family and in recent years even more Mannocks have been literally unearthed. During repairs in the parish church, a burial vault was found under the floor containing seven coffins. Two of them held plaques identifying them as belonging to Sir Thomas Mannock the 8th baronet who died in 1781 and to Teresa Mannock.

Tendring Hall was once occupied by the Tendrings. William de Tendring had a grant of a fair and market here from Edward I. After some changes it came into the possession of the Rowleys, first of whom was Admiral Sir William Rowley, Knight of the Bath. Tendring Hall has been described as 'a large mansion on a commanding eminence in an extensive and well-wooded park.' It was re-built in the 18th century of white brick with Portland stone dressings.

Common folk have also prospered here in the past and best remembered of these is the draper who became Sir William Capel and Lord Mayor of London but was never quite able to resist flamboyant gestures where money was concerned. Having lent the king, Henry VII, a great deal of money, he was so overcome with the honour of feasting with his royal debtor that he threw the bonds on to the fire. On another occasion this intolerable sycophant had a valuable pearl ground to powder and placed in a drink to toast the king's health.

Stonham Aspall

This is Stonham Aspall because it has to be differentiated from other Stonhams nearby. The name Aspall or Haspele belonged to the one-time lords of the manor here. The other Stonhams also have additions to the name. One is Stonham Earl, usually called Earl Stonham nowadays, because the lordship was once held by the Earl of Norfolk and afterwards by the Earl of Suffolk. The other Stonham accepts the designation Parva.

The village nestles among trees not far from the Norwich to Ipswich road and the vital institutions of Church, school and public house are assembled close together at the end of the main street. The church is modestly beautiful in a leafy setting in which stands an unusual alabaster monument to a member of the Wingfield family that for a long time occupied Broughton Hall nearby.

Proud of its range of ten bells and a record of expert campanology, the church must have made its presence heard if not felt in the village. It is not surprising that the public house has joined the cause and calls itself 'The Ten Bells'.

Stowlangtoft

An unassuming village with a long name, a mile or so south of Ixworth. Langtoft is added because it was the name of the lords of the manor here and Stow on its own, though much easier to say, could be with a little effort confused with Stowmarket.

Long after the Langtofts held the manor came the eminent family of d'Ewes. A wall monument in the church shows Paul d'Ewes kneeling, with his two wives and eight children. Little did he know that one of this brood of infants would become a famous antiquarian and scholar. This was Simon (sometimes given as Symond) who was made a baronet in 1641 and impressed everyone with a promise to re-write the history of England but seldom got beyond the title page. He spent years studying documents and records of the Tower of London and would have been happy to do no more than this but through loyalty to the Puritan cause served as a member of the Long Parliament until, rather to his relief, he was expelled with 40 others by Colonel Pride.

The church is believed to have been built on the site of a Roman camp by Robert Dacy of Ashfield. Roman remains have been found in the vicinity including a pot full of coins and not far off, a fine tesselated pavement. Before he died, the philanthropist and churchman, Robert Dacy, changed his name to that of his native village — Robert Ashfield.

Stutton

Not many decades ago the villagers of Stutton were viewing the future of the community with considerable misgiving. There were too few young people, too few houses, too few jobs. It all seemed to point to a slowly decaying life-style, with loss of amenities and possibly the closing of the school. Since then, happily, there has been a complete rejuvenation. New blood and new energy has brought hope and enthusiasm. Newcomers and old have joined in the resuscitation and a community council formed to direct ideas and projects.

The village has had its ups and downs. As far back as the plague, so the story goes, misfortune was near at hand. At that time the village was clustered about the church which is now some distance away from the centre. The legend tells that the old village was burnt down to stop the spread of the plague and that the victims were buried in that slightly ghostly avenue to the church called the Drift.

Another belief that persists is that there is coal in them there fields. Certainly a deep, exploratory shaft was sunk here in the 1890s but no more was heard of it. Rumour is that the project was smothered in the interests of local landowners who wanted to keep their pheasant shooting undisturbed.

There was a time when barges could come up the Stour and call at the wharf at Stutton Point to take on sugar beet and other agricultural produce. Although this is no longer possible, there is water enough nearby with the huge Alton reservoir filling a whole valley with the water needs of Ipswich and district. A near-casualty of the reservoir was the one remaining water-mill of the two formerly here. Its fate was widely discussed and finally solved by dismantling the mill and setting it up again as a fascinating museum piece in the Rural Life collection at Stowmarket.

There must have been a sigh of relief from church-goers when a proper organ was installed in 1902. From 1832 for several years music had been supplied by a barrel organ which played only 12 tunes. A great leap forward was made in 1840 when a second barrel-organ with another 12 tunes was added. Ten more years passed with the bulk of the tunes in the hymnal barely used and there was jubilation when a harmonium was installed in 1850.

Sudbourne ❧

Kings, nobles and millionaires have fired guns here; so have soldiers of the rank and file of the army. The occasions were obviously in no danger of overlapping and the pheasants and rabbits that were the objectives of the shooting parties of earlier days had little importance to the army except perhaps, as a stew.

From the beginning, Sudbourne was seen to be a fine resort for the hunting fraternity. In this village of scattered houses and enormous open spaces, game was encouraged to proliferate. Sudbourne Hall must have entertained the most prestigious shooting parties in the county. When the original Tudor hall was rebuilt, it was as a plain, quadrangular hunting lodge, though of mansion-like dimensions.

Rifle fire took over in the last war when the whole village came under the control of the military and was used for battle-ground training. Sudbourne was a lost village so far as the ordinary citizen was concerned and it was not a thing to enquire into too closely at that time.

The original Sudbourne Hall was built by Sir Michael Stanhope who was granted the manor. The Stanhope monument in the church shows him with a wife and two daughters. Underneath, the inscription tells that Sir Michael had served for 20 years as a gentleman of the Privy Chamber to Queen Elizabeth and until his death occupied the same confidential position under James I.

Perhaps the most important person to be associated with the village was Sir Richard Wallace. Apparently related in some way to the 4th Marquis of Hertford, who occupied the Hall, he was bequeathed the enormous wealth and vast art treasures which were to form the basis of the famous Wallace Collection in London.

Sutton

In my childhood, Sutton was a foreign land. We would look across the river Deben from the shore at Woodbridge and marvel at the woods and sloping fields on the other side. On special days we would be rowed across in the ferry boat to picnic there where savages were likely to attack and where pirates' treasure lay buried under every tree. Childish imagination is strong but it could not for a moment envisage the vast treasure that was later to be found in these fields.

Generally, of course, Sutton is reached by road over the bridge at Melton. Here are large, flat fields and the village looks stretched and lonely in the open landscape which is nevertheless well fringed with trees as windbreaks. There are footpaths two or three miles long from the road to the river where one can see in reverse the river view I saw as a child. One footpath leads the walker over private land to the area of Sutton Hoo, the site of the discovery of the famous burial ship.

Here, in the summer of 1939 when more pressing matters were occupying peoples' minds, was revealed the greatest archaeological treasure of England's history. One of a group of mounds was found to hold the remains of a Saxon burial ship. It was 82 feet long and was probably a rowing galley, built of wooden planks held by iron nails. Time had disposed of the wood but the nails and the impressions left by the timbers were clear to see. Most of the treasure lay on the floor in the centre of the ship, covered by rotted wood and sand. There were gold ornaments and buckles, a huge silver salver, a sword with a jewelled pommel and other objects, priceless from a historical as well as a monetary point of view.

Detailed study of the ship and the treasure led to the belief that, though it had all the signs of a Viking funeral, this was a Saxon burial and probably that of Raedwald, King of the East Angles, who died about 600 A.D.

Tattingstone 🐌

Squire White certainly left his mark on the village. Either from a sense of humour or for some reason of his own he created what is known as the Tattingstone Wonder. It has stood there since 1742 when Mr. White died and must have deceived a multitude of people in that time. It is a church – at least, to all appearances it is a church since it has a tower, ecclesiastical-looking windows and what seems to be nave and chancel. Closer attention shows that it is nothing of the kind, the tower has only three sides, there is a chimney or two and other signs of domestic rather than religious use. In fact, this reverential guise cloaks one or two cottages originally designed for Mr. White's employees. No doubt it all gave the squire a chuckle or two. 'People are often wondering at nothing,' he is supposed to have said, 'I'll give them something to wonder at.' He did not imagine that his Wonder would one day look across the road to another wonder – the great lake or reservoir of Alton Water, which fills what was once a valley of farmland.

An unmistakable village institution is St. Mary's Hospital, which has climbed out of the early opprobrium attached to it as a Victorian workhouse and does its important work in an enlightened atmosphere. An inmate of the old workhouse for something like 20 years was Mrs. Ann Candler, a woman who found release and hope in the writing of poetry. As a young bride she had been suddenly left destitute by her husband's desertion and had suffered considerable hardship before coming to St. Mary's. Fortunately for her, Ann Candler's poems came to the notice of Mrs. Elizabeth Cobbold, whose kindness and understanding was already known to others. Mrs. Cobbold became Ann's patroness and arranged for publication of her poems. With a sum of money so raised, Ann Candler was able to leave the workhouse for private lodgings at Holton near Stratford St. Mary, where she died in 1814 aged 74.

Theberton ✎

It is strange to think that this quiet, almost-forgotten village is inevitably associated with war and with warriors for there is nothing but kindness to be found here among the inhabitants. Even the churchyard bids the visitor welcome with the 'sitting stone' of old John Fenn, once rector of this parish. It is an altar tomb but invites the passer-by to sit on it. The church is old, with a Norman doorway and an odd, under-sized octagonal tower.

It was in June 1917 when war came violently to the village. An enemy airship came silently from the skies over the sea, faltering and drifting after attacks by British planes. It crashed eventually here at Theberton and in the churchyard now, within a special enclosure, are the 16 graves of the German dead. For a time they were 'unknown' but in later years names were found and this message inscribed: 'Who are thou that judgest another man's servant? To his own master he standeth or falleth.'

A fragment of the Zeppelin hangs in the church. Outside, near the village's memorial to its dead once stood a machine-gun in memory of that great soldier, Lieut. Col. Charles Hotham Montagu Doughty-Wylie, V.C., hero of many foreign campaigns before losing his life at Gallipoli. Col. Doughty-Wylie had already fought with Kitchener in the Sudan and was prominent in the battle for Omdurman on September 1st 1898. He was wounded in the Boer War and again in some uprising in Turkey where his bravery saved many lives.

In the bitter, tragic campaign of Gallipoli, Col. Doughty-Wylie led a night attack to try to capture a fort. The attack was successful but at the very moment that his troops were cheering, their leader was struck by a bullet and killed.

The family of Doughtys lived at the Hall, built at the end of the eighteenth century by George Doughty, a High Sheriff of Suffolk. It was enlarged in 1850 and allows a fine view of the sea three miles away.

Thornham ✎

The enchantment of Thornham, both Magna and Parva, lies in the profusion of its trees, once planted by the Henniker estate and now forming avenues of green shade along the quiet summer roads. They give a sense of peace and unworldliness that enfolds cottages and churches alike. The church of Thornham Magna, in particular, has an air of unruffled majesty with its crown of battlements and pinnacles against a backcloth of green. It contains monuments to a few of those who have left these lanes for fame and honour elsewhere and to the lords of the manor here, the succession of Lord Hennikers at the Hall. One memorial is to Robert Killigrew, who was a page of honour to Charles II and who welcomed both that monarch and Queen Elizabeth to this leafy retreat. Killigrew was a gallant soldier who became a brigadier-general but was fated to die on a foreign field at the battle of Almanza in 1707.

In keeping with the smaller village, the church of Parva is a fascinating miniature, with a queer little pointed tower that, like the nave, seems to have forgotten to grow bigger. Yet it has much of interest from its long history. Both doorways are Norman and both have kept well against the wear of centuries, as if time had no ill-effects in this charming place.

When I was young, the pride of Thornham Magna was the Hall, the Tudor residence of the Lords Henniker. Unhappily, time has not been so kind in this respect. By 1950 the Hall had become converted to a preparatory school and four years later, on a windy November night, fire broke out and the mansion became an inferno of flames. It was a sad sight for people for whom the Hall had always been the centre and the history of the village and sadder still in the morning light to discover that much of the ancient mansion was now but a charred ruin.

Thorpeness

Here was an ugly duckling of a village that was miraculously changed into a swan. A hundred years ago, Thorpe was an unconsidered hamlet of Aldringham, a community given over almost entirely to fishing. About 25 owners of local smacks governed the lives and the well-being of the total population. Spiritual guidance was provided by the Thorpe Fisherman's Bethel Hall, built in 1890. A photograph of the time shows the whole congregation in Sunday best standing outside the timber building,

WINDMILL AND
'HOUSE IN THE CLOUDS'
THORPENESS.

something like a hundred souls of all ages and probably the major part of the whole community.

The metamorphosis took place when the new century began and an imaginative planned named Stuart Ogilvy called in designers W. G. Wilson and F. Forbes Glennie to help him create a complete new holiday village. A landmark in the operation was the excavation of the famous Meare and at about the same time Thorpe took on another syllable to become Thorpeness.

The village itself consists of fairly modest-looking weather-boarded houses that fit in with the fishing tradition. Of much more interest to summer visitors is the Meare, about two miles along the coast road from Aldeburgh and an ideal boating lake for children. More surprising still is the edifice that has come to be known as 'The House in the Clouds'. Seeing it for the first time causes people to rub their eyes in disbelief. A house resting on the top of a square tower perhaps eighty feet high really looks like a 'House in the Clouds'. In fact, the 'house' at the top is a camouflaged water tank but the stem of the tower actually is a house and occupied by a family. Nearby is the post-mill which was brought here from Aldringham with the original intention of using it to pump water into the tank.

The Trimleys ❧

The Trimleys, with Walton also, form an almost continuous chain of houses along the three miles of what was until recently the only road in and out of Felixstowe. A new road, complete with round-about and flyover at Trimley St. Martin, now takes the port traffic on to the faster system which goes over the impressive Orwell Bridge and beyond without entering Ipswich.

Both Trimleys are extensive in area, reaching over a mile to the shoreline of the Orwell in one direction and almost within sight of the Deben in the other. At the Orwell foreshore, local inhabitants concerned about wildlife and footpaths, watch the expanding port of Felixstowe with alarm. Yet, despite such things as encroachment, increased traffic and the introduction of a fairly large housing estate in each of the parishes, there is still a predominantly rural atmosphere about the Trimleys.

Perhaps the most interesting feature here is the situation of the two churches, St. Mary and St. Martin, built close beside the road and separated by only a few yards of no-mans-land which forms the boundary of the two parishes. Persistent legend has it that the churches were built separately by two quarrelling sisters but local historians throw cold water on the idea. On the other hand, there seems to be no alternative explanation for the two churches to be rubbing shoulders in the same churchyard, so the theory of the warring sisters makes as good a story as any.

Both churches are ancient and at the present time offer a plain and even ugly appearance in contrast to those found in most villages. Nowadays the two are united as one parish, though in other respects St. Mary and St. Martin maintain their separate identities. The Civil War produced some degree of havoc, with the interiors of both churches desecrated and both rectors expelled for expressing sentiments contrary to the cause of Puritanism.

St. Martin, somewhat deeper into agricultural land than St. Mary, once had three windmills in service. Two of them were rather close together and the local joke is that one of these was demolished because the miller considered there was not enough wind for both.

At the corner of St. Martin's Green is displayed the very handsome village sign in the form of a portrait of Thomas Cavendish, Elizabethan sea-dog and local hero. Beneath the picture are the words attributed to him when far away from his native haunts.

'My God, said Thomas Cavendish, whatever may be-fall,
I'll ever love dear Trimley and the oaks at Grimston Hall.'

The Cavendish family had been lords of the manor at Grimston Hall nearby for over 300 years when young Thomas began to show his zest for adventure and the sea. No doubt he had heard and admired the stories of Francis Drake's perilous voyages and in due course Cavendish imitated his hero in many respects. Like Drake he had many encounters with the Spaniards and survived many a hard battle. With Sir Richard Grenville, he accompanied Raleigh across the sea to his new colony in America and soon after had the opportunity to do what he most wanted to do – to follow Drake's example and to become the second Englishman to sail round the world. In 1586 he fitted out three ships and sailed westwards, returning home triumphantly two years later to be received as a national hero.

Cavendish set off again in 1591 with five ships on a voyage that seemed to court disaster from start to finish. Only 15 of the 76 crewmen ever returned and Cavendish himself became separated from his little fleet to die alone in some foreign clime.

Tuddenham St. Martin 🌿

The wandering river Fynn crosses under the road bridge here at the lowest point of the village street. It is a pleasant walk to follow the river for a mile or so on either side of the road. The village is compactly housed with a variety of dwellings on both sides of the hill and all lies within the gentle ambience of the church of St. Martin. The church lends an ageless dignity to the street, standing on high ground as it does and with its 15th century west tower crowned with battlements. In the north wall is a well-preserved Norman doorway and inside is a font that is almost as old.

It has been reckoned that the font may be the most ancient in the county. It has an octagonal bowl with carvings of a variety of creatures and an elegant tall cover. Long-forgotten craftsmen have left their mark and a little of their lives here in the exquisite carving of bench-ends and modern craftsmen too have added their skill to the beautification of the church. A fine new chancel screen of oak taken from the windmills of Earl Soham and Ashfield was installed and dedicated at the end of the Second World War.

The east window tells a tragic tale of a young son of a rector, Alexander Paton, who lost his life soon after going to sea as a midshipman. On climbing a mast to secure a sail in a hurricane he was wrenched from his hold by the wind and lost in the sea. Another memorial is to Michael Wolversten, who fought gallantly for his king in the Civil Wars only to witness the monarch's execution. For his support of the Royalist cause, Wolversten lost his estates and almost his life by the brutal decrees of Cromwell.

Tunstall 🦢

It was once Tunstall-with-Dunningworth, a hamlet that is now completely lost save for Dunningworth Hall, but which once had its own church and rectory. There is a record of the church standing in 1520.

The church of Tunstall is a beautiful 14th century edifice embowered in trees, with many treasures surviving the gloating excesses of William Dowsing who — 'brake down 60 Superstitious Pictures' (probably in coloured glass) 'and broke in pieces the Rails; and gave orders to pull down the Steps.'

I suppose it would be possible for any village to make a rough graph of its changing fortunes in the last hundred years simply by using the figures of the school roll. At Tunstall they are certainly revealing:

(At opening)	1873	37 pupils
	1887	75 — but attendance erratic.
	1904	143
	1928	84
	1973	36

The school is now closed.

The first and last figures of a hundred years show almost exactly the same number of pupils. But at the beginning of the century the school was bursting its sides, having doubled the roll in 17 years. How can one account for the rapid decline in the early twenties? Perhaps a combination of Great War losses, smaller families and the general drift from the land can explain it, for there was at that time no great use of farm machinery to reduce the number of workers.

For many years soil experiments were carried on here, mainly to investigate the effects of the use of lime and chalk on light lands, a project that was eventually taken over by the firm of Fisons.

Ufford ❧

This is another village with two communities. They were once called Upper Street and Lower Street and were about half a mile apart. Now, the term Lower Ufford applies to the part which is in fact the more important. This is the old village, with 15th century houses and an even earlier church huddling together close to the street and quaint enough to attract many visitors on summer days. The Post Office is here, giving a kind of authority to Lower Ufford and nearby is the road bridge over the narrowing river Deben, probably the original ford of Uffa.

Uffa was a Scandinavian invader who settled here in the 5th century. He was important, perhaps a king, because the Venerable Bede talks of Uffa and of Redwald, king of the East Angles, in the same breath. He also mentions the ford between the royal palace at Rendlesham and the settlement at Eyke. After the Norman Conquest, the Peyton family arrived from Peyton Hall at Ramsholt and took the name of Ufford. Robert de Ufford was Chief Justice of Ireland in 1269 and his son was created a baron in 1337.

Ufford's ancient church, which shows herring-bone courses of ironstone from the local crag as well as sections of Caen stone, is generally believed to belong to the 12th century. Additions were made by Robert de Ufford and by the Willoughbys who succeeded to the Ufford estates on the death of the last male of the line.

The tower of this beautiful church faces up a short lane, its battlements majestic above the tall-chimneyed houses below. Inside, its greatest treasure is the great font cover, surely the most elaborate in Suffolk and perhaps in the whole country. Some have asserted that there is no other like it in the world. It was certainly impressive enough to deter Dowsing, who came with his minions on two occasions in 1648 but ordered that the cover should be spared. It is 18 feet high and seems to reach almost to the roof in a decorative cone of exquisite workmanship. It was made over 500 years ago, no doubt with pride and joy at the creation of this masterpiece of skill and beauty and it has given delight to worshippers and visitors ever since.

The High Street is now spared the thunder of traffic that for years took this route past the Crown Inn and the roadside houses. Now, the Crown has regained some of the peaceful charm more in keeping with its age. It was mentioned as long ago as 1524 and even today retains some of the features of its early days including a cheery and friendly atmosphere in the bars.

An Ufford divine who must not be overlooked in any account of the village was the Rev. Richard Lovekin. He was rector from 1621 to 1678, at which date he became 110 years old. A ripe old age even for a clergyman, though these seemed to survive better than most in those early days. The remarkable thing is that he was performing all his church and pastoral duties to the Sunday before his death. A story connected with the rector's earlier years was that, during the course of the Civil War he was robbed of everything he possessed except for a single silver spoon which he hid in his sleeve.

Walberswick ✺

That agricultural Suffolk would become a haven for artists and craftsmen would have seemed very unlikely years ago. Now, it is home for actors and writers, potters and painters, all with an avowed interest in the county. Perhaps it was Benjamin Britten and the Aldeburgh Festival that pointed the way and a desire for a more placid way of life that compelled people to follow. The whiff of the sea in old fishing villages has been one strong call to artistic instincts and it is not difficult to understand the popularity of such places as Walberswick.

Walberswick was a fishing and shipping centre of some importance at the time that Dunwich and Blythburgh were also flourishing. In 1450 there were 13 barques trading with Iceland and the Faroe Islands while as many as 22 fishing boats were setting off from and landing on these beaches. Tradition kept men fishing during the long decline and there is tragic evidence that it was being followed in strength up to the end of the last century. A memorial in the church tells of 'Seven Fishermen, Parishioners of Walberswick, who were drowned at Sea, Sept. 30 1883.'

When the first small, thatched church was demolished in 1473, a magnificent new one was built, 124 feet long and with a tower 90 feet high, with two aisles and two altars. It was fitting that such a prosperous village should have a church of majestic size, in particular to receive the prayers for those at sea. Then, as the fishing declined, so did the church's congregation. In 1585 the great bell of 1700 pounds in weight was sold and a hundred years later a new and more modest church was fashioned out of the old.

The decline of Walberswick was hastened, as it was at Dunwich, by a series of fires suspected to be arson, in the 17th and 18th centuries. There were other problems too. In 1590 the manor came into the possession of Sir Robert Broke, who promptly took away the common land belonging to the villagers. Amid great bitterness the land was regained some years later but the power struggle continued with cattle being driven off the common by the squire's employees. In the end it came to a brutal, stand-up fight between the squire's henchmen and the local commoners exasperated to the limit. In the battle four men were killed. The place where the fight took place was afterwards named Bloody Marsh.

The Waldingfields

In the spacious, heavy-land countryside between Sudbury and Lavenham lie the Waldingfields, Great and Little. The description of 'Little' is scarcely fair in these days since a post-war surge in new housing has elevated its importance very considerably. Yet, Waldingfield the Great may still have most to offer, particularly in regard to the church. St. Lawrence was built in the 14th century with a handsome tower and south porch and a beautiful east window of stained glass. It also shows an advantage from the vast attentions it received between 1836 and 1839, bringing a rejuvenated interior with new features including an increased seating capacity and with old monotones revitalised with paint. Now, there are hosts of details to admire, particularly in the chancel where some of the carving is reputed to be by Grinling Gibbons. There are some fine monuments to the Kedington family, once lords of the manor.

It is appropriate that one of the most revered names in church practice belonged to a man who was vicar here. John Hopkins, with Thomas Sternfield at his side, produced the metrical version of the

Psalms, a volume that ranks with the Bible and Prayer-book as being of universal fame.

Walpole 🌿

The road south-west from Halesworth goes through some of the best of our farming land to find the modest village of Walpole. A Norman doorway guards the ancient church and within there is a beautiful Jacobean altar-table but for once it is a chapel rather than a church that claims attention. It is believed to be the oldest but one in the whole country, having been established in 1646 for Congregational worshippers after having already served for 40 years as a meeting-house.

The old building is well-preserved, both inside and out and seems to have been constructed around the main support of a stout mast brought from a ship at Yarmouth. The mast and the galleries around give a brief impression of being in an old-time sailing vessel but this is soon superseded by a feeling of awe that this simple chapel knew village life in the time of Cromwell and all through the 300 years since. Political change and social change has all been distilled here into an individual need to offer prayer.

Walpole has reason to remember one of its sons. George Carver came from a poor family in the village and found it expedient, as did many others at that time, to leave home early to seek his fortune. In a shrewd and energetic life-time he came, indeed, to be a wealthy man. When he retired, he came back to Walpole to spend his fortune on supplying some of the needs whose absence in his own boyhood he could remember so well. Among his gifts are the almshouses for widows that would remedy for many women the hardship that his own mother knew.

Walsham-le-Willows 🌿

The position on the map of Walsham-le-Willows suggests a distinct aversion to town life since it is in the very centre of the square formed by Diss, Thetford, Bury St. Edmunds and Stowmarket and is about 11 miles from each. Visitors to the village may well feel that it has good reason to remain aloof. It has many picturesque houses, some thatched and timbered, an ancient inn and a very noble-looking church. The tower of St. Mary is particularly striking with its chequered pattern of flints surmounted by proud battlements and high pinnacles. The spacious interior of the church was cleaned and beautified in 1843, when some ancient wall paintings were discovered under the many coats of whitewash. There is also a stone plaque that was once of romantic interest to village maidens who would hang garlands upon it.

No doubt the church was well-attended in 1767 when small-pox threatened. Surprisingly, the medical resources of the time seemed to feel that they were more than equal to the occasion, a point of view partly explained by the vast profits which could be made. Notices were displayed advising everyone to be inoculated or suffer dire consequences. Two surgeons and an apothecary were standing by to provide the service. 'Ladies and Gentlemen', in the significance of these terms at that time, could receive attention in private cubicles for a fee of 5 guineas each. 'Servants and Others' were attended to with less ceremony for 2½ to 4 guineas. These substantial sums were required at the time of the inoculations and the surgeons betrayed some lack of faith in their own treatment, perhaps, in refusing credit.

Wangford 🪶

The unmistakable sheet of water that signals the turn-offs from the A12 to Southwold on the right and to Beccles on the left some halfway from Saxmundham to Yarmouth, also indicates the edge of the hamlet of Henham, formerly regarded as a twin 'township' with Wangford. Wangford is a mile or so further on, a large village beside a tributary of the river Blythe. Somehow it seems to have discarded Henham, though this covers the larger area and was once a hamlet in its own right.

Much of the land comprises the estate of Henham Hall, home of the Earls of Stradbroke and the population of 128 in the last century no doubt consisted chiefly of employees and tenants. The present Henham Hall is a magnificent 18th century mansion, the earlier Hall having been burnt down in 1773. The lordships of Wangford and Henham came to the Rous family, ancestors of the Earls of Stradbroke, in the reign of Henry VIII. Even older than the noble

160

family are many of the majestic oaks that have always graced the thousand-acre Henham Park, though 1100 of them were felled in 1842.

There was a priory of Cluniac monks here in early times which was granted at the Dissolution of the Monasteries to the Duke of Norfolk and sold by his son to Sir John Rous. The church of Wangford is built partly of brick, partly of flint and has an unusual spire steeple. Unlike so many other of our communities, the village seems to be disproportionately large for this small church.

Westhorpe ✑

How can it have been? In this sober, scattered parish who can imagine that there were once nobles and courtiers, a handsome Duke and a young Queen of France? Were there ever masques and balls and splendid Tudor revelry at the Hall? Indeed, was there ever a Hall?

It seems unlikely enough, yet the history books tell us that it was so. Westhorpe was a manor of the Dukes of Suffolk. In the 16th century it came to Charles Brandon, despite an error by an earlier Duke which cost him his head and the forfeiture of the estates. Charles Brandon, Duke of Suffolk received the estates back and lived in splendour at Westhorpe Hall and at Court. He had married twice and was alone again when the royal romance developed.

Mary Tudor, beautiful young sister of Henry VIII whom the Duke of Suffolk must have met at Court, had to subdue any personal desires of her own to satisfy the king's wish to placate France by marrying her to the aged king. In the year 1514 when she was eighteen, Mary Tudor married Louis XII in October and was crowned Queen of France in November. At the end of December her husband died and she returned to England to fly to the arms of Charles Brandon, whom she married without delay. The couple lived at Westhorpe in great style until she died. Sister of Henry VIII and Dowager Queen of France though she was, she was buried simply in the abbey church at Bury St. Edmunds but was later moved to the church of St. Mary's after the Dissolution of the Monastery. There was no memorial until 1758, when a plaque was placed on her tomb beside the altar. Nor is there anything left at Westhorpe of that great Tudor romance except for a royal pew in the church, a small tablet on the wall and a window carrying the fading coat-of-arms of the Suffolk family.

Westleton

Here is a fine, spacious green in a triangle that slopes upwards to its apex. A few houses jostle along the sides and at the base is the White Horse Inn and a shady pond on which the ducks paddle. Like so many villages along the coast it has a slightly desolate air as if remembering, even in summer, the harsh winds from the sea.

Some of the houses, modernised and improved though they now are, were the homes of humble fishermen for there was little but fishing and farm-work to sustain life in days gone by. Once, nearly every cottage had a small brick kiln in the garden in which herrings were cured over smoking oak chips and for a time much store was placed on this cottage industry.

Westleton is one of our largest villages but is unusual in having no great mansion or hall of the kind that used to dominate most rural communities. Independence must have cost the locals dear since there were no hand-outs from the gentry and none of those benevolences and bequests that played quite an important part in well-endowed villages. The House of Industry at Bulcamp had no shortage of inmates. In the poverty that followed the Napoleonic Wars, it was not a rare thing for a couple to marry and enter the workhouse with their children born into the system.

In the Middle Ages the village was prosperous since it was an important stage on the road to the flourishing port of Dunwich. When the port declined, the heavy waggons no longer rumbled by the green and horsemen came but rarely to the inn. At about that time it became the responsibility of the village to maintain its own piece of turnpike. Two toll houses were built and the right was granted to charge all travellers (except the Royal Family who conceivably could well have afforded it) toll for the privilege of passing over that stretch of road. The passage of animals too, required dues and some frantic counting must have gone on sometimes at the fixed rate of 5d. a score. No doubt round figures were generally acceptable rather than mathematical exactness.

Wetheringsett

The village nestles in a hollow in which all its features are close at hand. Here is the school, the church, the manor house and miniature post-office, with a close-knit collection of houses in between. It has the look of a perfect old-time village, unworried by traffic and other modern frenzies and set in a landscape of magnificent trees. At the very base of the hollow is a little stream, a tributary of the river Dove that actually forms a runnel beneath one of the houses.

Though the village is closely encircled by agricultural land, there is a scattering of houses along the completely rural Green Lane, and over a mile away, a separate and apparently independent hamlet called Wetherup, which has no official recognition as such.

The church here has seen manorial lords and churchmen a-plenty since its origin in the 14th century but none more memorable than a rector installed here in 1590. His name was Richard Hakluyt. At the peak of Elizabethan greatness, when explorers were delving into unknown corners of the world, Hakluyt set himself the task of recording and narrating the stories of all the major voyages that had ever taken place. His finished work is generally known as Hakluyt's *Voyages* but was in fact called a *Book of Navigations, Voyages, Traffiques and Discoveries of the English Nation.*

In the 26 years of his life at Wetheringsett, Hakluyt re-lived the excitement and dangers of seamen, merchants and adventurers as he followed the details of their voyages. From his earliest years in London and at Westminster School, he had been intensely interested in travel and exploration and concerned that so little was known generally of the achievements of brave men in their tiny ships. Perhaps his first enthusiasm was aroused by a relative who had rooms in London and who provided a kind of communication service for merchants and sailors regarding ships and cargoes. From this rose a yearning to know more of destinations and discoveries and the only way he could learn of such adventures was to travel to seaports to interview sailors and to way-lay captains and admirals in their haunts in London in order to record their stories. Hakluyt came to be known to all the great Elizabethan explorers and was a personal friend of Raleigh and Drake.

In close support of his enthusiasm for the voyages of others was his keen patriotism, provoked while in France by what he considered to be French denigration of England. In his great work, he determined to show that his countrymen were both adventurous and enterprising.

Wherstead 🦢

Wherstead lies beside the Orwell close to the western end of the new and impressive Orwell Bridge. The great house of Wherstead Park was built in 1792 by Sir Robert Harland who occupied it for a considerable number of years before letting it to Lord Granville. The attraction for the noble lord was the abundance of game and the house was used for numerous shooting parties. On one occasion, a shot from the gun wielded by the Duke of Wellington caught Lord Granville in the side of the face. While the pellets – eleven had penetrated his cheek and chin – were being removed, the Duke was cursing and confounding the noble features for being in front of his gun.

The amount of game on the estate inevitably attracted poachers. One night a gang of about twelve gathered on the Strand beside the river but vigilant gamekeepers followed their movements while Sir Robert sent a message to Ipswich to turn out the Dragoons. Very soon the poachers were surrounded and the situation so desperate for them that some tried swimming across the river to escape.

In 1803 an earthen pot containing 2000 Roman coins was turned up by a ploughman and handed to Sir Robert who forthwith chalked up on his front door – THE ROMAN BANK. Further extensive digging in the area brought forth a good deal of Roman pottery but no more treasure.

An interesting story is told here relating to the early introduction of tea to genteel households. Lady Harland had come into possession of a quantity of tea and kindly took half a pound to the wife of a tenant farmer. Unwilling to admit her ignorance of teamaking, the puzzled farm-wife tipped the half-pound into a saucepan and boiled it up. She confessed later to Lady Harland that she found that tea was not entirely to her taste.

Wickham Market ❧

There is no mistaking the centre of Wickham Market. The entire activity of the place devolves upon the little square where shoppers' cars are ever chock-a-block and a bus shelter and toilets take up what space is left. From across the street the White Hart Hotel looks down perhaps is some relief now that the by-pass has siphoned off some of the heavy traffic from the narrow roads. Nearby is the handsome church, renowned for its tell-tale spire that forms a landmark – and a sea-mark too, I understand – for the uncertain traveller. Perhaps because by contrast most of our churches are square-towered, the spire attracts much admiration. In fact, it is only about 70 feet high but has the benefit of being situated on an eminence and without much opposition from other buildings.

Everyone knows of the market here. It was originally granted by Henry VI in 1440 and the weekly event has probably continued without major breaks ever since. It still goes on, although the type of merchandise has changed somewhat. Mondays in this part of Suffolk would not be the same without it.

There was once a Shire Hall here, a superior edifice in which was held the Quarter Sessions. When the Sessions were moved to Woodbridge, the lord of the manor of the time decided that the Shire Hall had no further use and proceeded to demolish it. The building materials were taken for the building of a farmhouse in Letheringham.

Perhaps the most notable character of Wickham Market's past was John Kirby, whose *Suffolk Traveller*, based on his exhaustive surveys of the county in 1732 to 1734, forms such a valuable reference to village life in those days.

Wingfield ❧

The expanding power of the de la Pole family found a perfect setting for their ambitions here at Wingfield. Already they had made fortunes as merchants despite humble beginnings in the north and in 1331 William de la Pole became the first mayor of the city of Hull. When the de la Poles moved south to Suffolk, the manor and fortunes of the long-established Wingfield family was in the keeping

of the heiress, Katherine Wingfield. At the marriage of Katherine to
Michael de la Pole, the great name of Wingfield was lost to the
village. They had been here since the days of the Conqueror and at
one time boasted eight knights in the family, two of them with
Orders of the Garter.

Soon the de la Poles became Dukes and Earls of Suffolk and
Michael obtained a licence from the king to convert the manor
house into a castle. It looks grand enough still in this quiet corner of
the village beside the great common, with a moat and a causeway to
the front entrance. On certain days of the year it is open to the
public.

Church, college and inn rub shoulders at the top end of the
village. The 14th century church is framed in trees and carries many
memorials to the powerful families who have lived here, among
them William de la Pole, first Duke of Suffolk and friend of the king,
who led the English armies triumphantly in the French wars until
defeated by the Maid of Orleans. Blamed afterwards for some of the
ills of the nation at that time, he was impeached and banished but
was brutally murdered by his enemies on the voyage.

The College stands beside the church. It was first erected about
the year 1362 by the Wingfields for a master and nine priests.
Nearby, in keeping with the sense of early feudal power in these
parts, the inn is still called the De La Pole Arms.

Witnesham

Witnesham straggles for two or three miles along the road between
Ipswich and Debenham. There are two long and (for Suffolk) quite
steep hills with some consolidation of housing in each valley.
Perhaps it is reasonable to see the village centre as being at the first
valley where an S bend shows a fair collection of dwellings and the
public house. The Barley Mow is well-known in these parts and
sometimes in other parts too as it occasionally features in the
cartoons of Giles, who lives nearby.

The second valley, called the Burwash, has another group of
houses and a lane that leads off to the church but the village goes on
to a further housing estate at the top of the hill and close to the
border with Swilland, where the former Area School spreads itself
across the head of a meadow.

The Area School was not the first in the village. As long ago as 1840 there was a voluntary National School, largely financed and run by a kindly rector. It was at the beginning of the centralisation in rural districts in the 1930s that Area Schools were deployed in chosen situations to take the children from several villages. In the years that I knew the school, in the 1940s and 1950s, children arrived from about seven villages round about, all on foot or on 'Committee' bicycles. (The Education Committee later became the Local Education Authority.) At that time children stayed at the school from the age of five to fifteen, until further centralisation destroyed this happy state of affairs and took the older children off to schools elsewhere. A Horticultural Centre was then set up here where it could make use of vacant facilities and provide courses and training in the scientific aspects of gardening.

At this north end of the village is also the moated Tudor mansion of Berghersh House, for long years the home of the Berghersh family after Sir Bartolomew Berghersh arrived in the reign of Edward III. By chance, the same king saw the first arrivals of the Meadows family, seated here ever since that time. At Witnesham Hall, just beyond the church and close by the spot where the Fynn begins its meandering course to the Deben, was born the famous naturalist, William Kirby. Kirby was no great explorer but saw the wonder of the nature that was close at hand, removing himself only to the neighbouring village of Barham where he stayed as rector for the whole of his long life.

The church of St. Mary occupies a peaceful spot beside the lane, with its embattled tower ageless against the moving clouds. Among so many others resting here are four rectors with an average of 50 years of service each to the community. For many years the tower hummed with the activity of swarms of bees that made their home there. A shrewd pair of Muscovy ducks seized upon the idea and used the loft over the porch to nest and rear their chicks. The solution to the problem of getting chicks down to earth was never witnessed but it is believed that they were ferried down on the mother's back.

Woolpit ✒

The distant past from which legends arise provides Woolpit with stranger stories than most villages can claim. There were wolf-pits here, we are told, as long as a thousand years ago that were intended for the destruction of wolves. It is an idea that raises many questions in modern minds and stretches the imagination rather more than we normally allow. When we hear that, centuries later, small green children emerged from the wolf-pits we are inclined to view another phenomenon here with justifiable doubt. This was the spring called Lady's Well in a meadow by the church and once believed to be of great curative powers, particularly for sore eyes. Perhaps sore eyes were prevalent then for tradition tells of many pilgrims who came to a chapel beside the spring.

Wolves, green children and perhaps even people with sore eyes are notably absent from modern Woolpit which, like many other villages in recent years, has been by-passed by a new road system and left in comparative peace. It is never like the golden days of yore, of course; traffic is reduced but not banished. Nevertheless, there is time and space enough to admire the many kinds of homes here, from the straightforward modern to the picturesque, timbered Weaver House. Flint and brick, timber and thatch co-habit here in complete harmony. Some of the buildings, including the Swan Inn and the Bull, are listed as being of special architectural and historic interest. Just opposite the ancient Village Institute is the village pump, now grandly roofed and pillared as a memento of days gone by.

Woolverstone ✒

William Berners had already left his name upon a London street when he came to settle in Woolverstone. It was a happy choice, for of the many mansions built in the 18th century, few can have been more felicitously situated. Woolverstone lies on the quiet peninsula between the Orwell and the Stour, a few miles from the sea and not far from what nowadays is termed 'Constable country'. There were 400 acres of Parkland, well-wooded and stocked with spotted deer. In front of the Hall the grounds slope down to the foreshore of the Orwell and there are splendid views from the Hall of the estuary and of the Nacton shore opposite, where another great house, Orwell Park, can be seen.

The Hall is beautifully proportioned and spacious with extensive wings to the main edifice connected by colonnades. It is built of Woolpit brick and is impressive with Ionic columns. The Berners are remembered by an obelisk set up in the park. William and his wife both died in the same year and their son Charles erected this monument, almost 100 feet high, in 1793. Also in the park is the handsome little church of St. Michael, restored by Sir Gilbert Scott in 1832. Stone monkeys have always guarded the gateway to the park and also the almshouses nearby, built by the Berners. They are believed to have had some special significance for the Berners family since the monkey is incorporated into their crest.

Another animal mentioned here is the cat belonging to the Cat House, whose painted walls and white figure of a cat on the window-sill looks somewhat strange in this rural spot. The house was a haunt of smugglers, according to local tradition, and the white cat a signal to the shore.

At the end of the last war the Hall came into the possession of the London County Council, whose original idea was to transfer the London Nautical School here for the benefit of boys of exceptional promise. It is now a boarding school for boys from London boroughs.

Wortham ꙮ

The Wortham of the last century is clearly illuminated for us by the keen eyes and kindly judgment of the Rev. Richard Cobbold, rector here for 52 years. The rector was of a literary turn of mind and published many poems and other works, including the Suffolk classic, *Margaret Catchpole*.

Cobbold came to the village with a heavy heart, as he admits in his account of his ministrations here. He was unwilling to leave the cosy social round in Ipswich where he had been curate at St. Mary-le-Tower. Wortham seemed remote and unattractive by contrast but there was no gain-saying the wishes of the bishop. Fortunately, the mood of despair soon changed and he became absorbed in the real needs of the parish while his prevailing relaxation was to record in words and sketches all the features and characters of the village that he came to love.

169

He writes of the day when he heard of his favourite brother's death in a London hotel bedroom and he came to the Rectory Fields to look down on the village and the church – 'that ancient structure with the Old Round Tower.' With grief past, he turned again to his shrewd portrayals of the community. There was not one cottager so slight or unimportant that he did not become a character in Cobbold's gallery.

The oldest Wortham family, now extinct, was that of Betts or Bettes. Generation after generation of them lived at The Hall, Wortham (which is distinct from Wortham Hall). The name occurs in the first church register of 1535 and in fact the Betts arrived in the village in 1490. An odd coincidence has been found in these figures and the life-span of the Betts dynasty. From 1490 another 414 years would have to elapse before the same figures came together again – that is, 1904. It was in that year that Katherine Betts died and ended the family line.

An odd situation arose in 1830 in connection with the Dolphin Inn, so exactly on the border with Burgate that when beating the bounds it was usual to follow the line into the front door and out of the back. A boy of 13 had lived at the Dolphin for a time and on becoming a pauper presented the Poor Law Officers with a poser as to whether he was the responsibility of Wortham or Burgate. The bedroom he had slept in was situated across the border line and it was decided that it all depended on the position of the bed. Here again, there was a problem for the bed had been over the very beam that indicated the boundary. Calculations eventually revealed that the boy had been 5 inches in Wortham and the rest of him in Burgate.

One might expect from this that the onus of charity fell upon Burgate but when the case was presented it was decided that the pauper had no claim upon either parish because he had not been fully in one or the other.

Wrentham

Was it the motor-car that finally destroyed the integrated way of village life? Certainly the old-style ways survived well into the present century and up to the Great War. Even in the 1920s the blacksmiths and wheelwrights were busy, the local builder was content to push a handcart to deal with his commitments nearby, the shoemaker and the tailor could rely on farmers and gentry for regular orders. With the coming of the car the indigenous economy was forsaken and the village tradesmen driven away to be replaced by a new-style countryman with no real part in the basic way of rural life.

Wrentham is a large village a mile or so from the sea and just north of Southwold. With fishing and farming on its door-step it was once a thriving community in its own right. A century ago about 50 people – which in those days probably represented 50 families – were industriously engaged in keeping the village as an independent unit. There were three blacksmiths and three brick-layers (and three beerhouses) four shoemakers and four grocers and drapers. There were two surgeons, two carpenters, two tailors, two land agents, two watch-repairers, a saddler, sawyer, plumber, cooper, miller and wheelwright.

Wrentham supported itself in other ways too. A whole generation before compulsory education arrived there were two voluntary schools, a National and a British. The National school was built in 1834 at a cost of £745-14-5, raised chiefly by contributions from the lord of the manor downwards to the cottage dweller, with grants from the Treasury and the National Schools Society. About 100 pupils attended whenever the demands of farm-work allowed, and they paid a fee of one penny a week. The British school, erected in 1837, provided for about 50 pupils.

Yaxley

A very handsome and substantial village sign greets the visitor to Yaxley, close to the old Roman road between Ipswich and Nor-wich. The sign depicts a bird against a leafy background and apparently perching on a large wheel. The wheel looks like a compass face or a horoscope chart. It is certainly a bit of a puzzle.

A few enquiries reveal that the bird is a cuckoo and is displayed because that is believed to be the meaning of the name Yaxley. The circle is a 'sexton's wheel' and the most erudite may be forgiven for looking blank at this information since, apart from one at Long Stratton at the Norfolk end of the same road, Yaxley has the only one in the country.

A description of the 'sexton's wheel', believed to be of the 15th century, says that it consists of two wheels which are 2 feet 8 inches in diameter, revolving on the same axle. The wheels are marked with the six days sacred to the Blessed Virgin and at each of these points is a small hole to which a short piece of string is attached. 'Whenever a devout person was desirous of keeping a penance by fasting, he applied to the sexton to set the wheels spinning and whichever string he caught decided the day to begin the fast.'

The 'sexton's wheel' was found in separate parts in 1867 by the Rev. W. H. Sewell in a room above the south porch of the church. It was exhibited as a mystery object to a meeting of archaeologists at Bury St. Edmunds in 1869. Many theories were advanced about its use, including the idea that the wheels were merely for ornamenting church doors. However, some verses were discovered which promised to show some light, as in the lines:

'The Sexton turns the wheel about and bids the stander-by
To hold the thread whereby he doth, the time and season try.'

Later, this theory was challenged again when it was suggested that the wheel is similar to the bell wheels used at Mass in Spain. It could well have been used as a bell wheel in pre-Reformation days.

Yoxford 🌿

Travellers on the old Roman road from central Suffolk to the coast join up with the main A12 to Lowestoft and beyond in the middle of Yoxford. The village hugs the junction, with most of the houses lining the approach road along the valley of the river Yox (which becomes the Minsmere at neighbouring Middleton).

No doubt with some reason the village gained the title of The Garden of Suffolk at some time in the past. It may be that it refers to the gardens of the great houses here for there are three mansions with extensive grounds. In earlier days they must have absorbed the labour of most of the village. There is Grove Park, well named for its setting among trees on the south side while the Rookery or Rookery Park has been justly proud of its gardens framed in ancient yew hedges. Cockfield Hall, a mansion of Tudor origin with much restoration, is Yoxford's direct association with a great event of history.

Here was kept under close guard by order of Queen Elizabeth herself the unhappy sister of Lady Jane Grey, the Nine Days Queen. Lady Katherine Grey, married on the same day as her sister, had already suffered the pain of being deserted by her first husband and separated from her second. She spent the rest of her life at Cockfield Hall, was buried in the parish church but later removed to the more august precincts of Salisbury Cathedral. The saddest day of her life must have been that before her sister's execution when she received a pathetic letter from her recommending the balm of religious faith.

Perhaps it was the garden of the old Three Tuns inn that earned the epithet of the Garden of Suffolk. This was a famous hostelry said to have had the names of Nelson and of Dickens in its visitors' book but which was unfortunately burnt to the ground about 1926. In its heyday it maintained a plot of ground on the opposite side of the road as a flower garden and its bright summer colours must have caught the eye and the admiration of all passers-by.

There are memorials here to Charles Blois, wounded at Waterloo; to David Elisha Davy who lost his wealth in the depression that followed the Napoleonic Wars but finished his scholarly history of the county while in 'exile' at Ufford; to Ann Candler, born in a poor family, who taught herself to read and write and who, in a sojourn of many years in a workhouse, wrote many poems of merit enough to secure help and comfort in her old age.

At the peak of Yoxford's prosperity around 1869 when its population had increased from 800 in 1801 to about 1300, a gazetteer gave this description of the village: 'It is situated in a remarkably pleasant neighbourhood, surrounded by beautiful country, interspersed with many seats of the gentry and is lighted by gas.' Of such things is the village story made.

Index

Alderton 9
Aldham 10
Aldringham 11
Aspall 12
Assington 13

Barham 14
Barningham 15
Barrow 16
Barsham 17
Barton Mills 19
Battisford 20
Bedingfield 21
Benacre 22
Benhall 23
Bentley 24
Blundeston 24
Blythburgh 25
Botesdale 28
Boulge 29
Bradfield Combust 30
Bramfield 32
Bramford 33
Brandeston 34
Brightwell 35
Bromeswell 36
Bures 37
Butley 38
Buxhall 39

Campsea Ash 40
Cavendish 41
Chelsworth 43
Clare 44
Claydon 45
Cockfield 46
Coddenham 47
Cookley 48

Covehithe 49
The Creetings 49
Culford 50

Dalham 51
Darsham 52
Dennington 53
Denston 54
Dunwich 56

Earl Soham 57
East Bergholt 58
Easton 60
Elmswell 61
Elveden 61
Erwarton 62
Euston 63

Fakenham 65
Farnham 66
Felsham 66
Finningham 67
Flixton 68
Fornham 69
Framlingham 70
Fressingfield 72
Freston 73

Gipping 74
Glemsford 75
Great Bealings 76
Great Blakenham 77
Groton 78
Grundisburgh 79

Hasketon 81
Hawstead 81
Helmingham 82
Hemingstone 84
Hengrave 85

Heveningham 86
Hintlesham 87
Hitcham 88
Holbrook 88
Hollesley 89
Honington 90
Hoxne 91

Icklingham 92
Ickworth 93

Kedington 94
Kelsale 95
Kersey 96
Kesgrave 97
Kessingland 98
Kirton 99
Knodishall 100

Lavenham 101
Laxfield 102
Letheringham 103
Lidgate 104
Long Melford 105

Martlesham 107
Mellis 108
Melton 109
Mendlesham 110
Mettingham 112
Middleton 112
Monk Soham 114

Nacton 114
Nayland 116
Needham Market 117
Newbourne 117
Norton 118

Offton 119
Orford 119
Otley 122
Oulton 123

Palgrave 124
Parham 125
Peasenhall 126
Pin Mill 126
Playford 128
Polstead 129

Rattlesden 130
Redgrave 131
Rendlesham 132
Rickinghall 133
Rushbrooke 134
Rushmere St. Andrew 135

Sibton 136
Snape 137
Somerleyton 139
Sotterley 141
The Southelmhams 141
Stanton 142
Stoke-by-Clare 143
Stoke-by-Nayland 144
Stonham Aspall 145
Stowlangtoft 145
Stutton 146
Sudbourne 147
Sutton 148

Tattingstone 149
Theberton 150
Thornham 150
Thorpeness 151
The Trimleys 153
Tuddenham St. Martin 154
Tunstall 155

Ufford   156

Walberswick   157
The Waldingfields   158
Walpole   159
Walsham-le-Willows   159
Wangford   160
Westhorpe   161
Westleton   162
Wetheringsett   163
Wherstead   164

Wickham Market   165
Wingfield   165
Witnesham   166
Woolpit   168
Woolverstone   168
Wortham   169
Wrentham   170

Yaxley   171
Yoxford   172